THE GENERAL KNOWLEDGE QUIZ BOOK

Derek O'Brien was born in Kolkata. He began his career as a journalist for *Sportsworld* magazine but soon shifted to advertising. After working for a number of very successful years as Creative Head of Ogilvy, Derek decided to focus all his energy and talent in his passion—quizzing.

Derek soon became Asia's best-known quizmaster and the CEO of Derek O'Brien & Associates. He has been the host of the longest-running game show on Indian television, the *Cadbury Bournvita Quiz Contest*, for which he was voted the Best Anchor of a Game Show at the Indian Television Academy Awards for three years in a row. Always innovating, Derek is also credited with having conducted the first quiz on Twitter in 2010.

Derek has written over fifty bestselling reference, quiz and textbooks. In 2017, he was re-elected to the Rajya Sabha as a Member of Parliament (MP) for a second term. He is the Leader of the All India Trinamool Congress Parliamentary Party in the Rajya Sabha and the chief national spokesperson of the party.

Keep in touch with Derek on Twitter, where his handle is @derekobrienmp, and on Facebook at www.facebook.com/MPDerekOBrien/

Other books by Derek O'Brien
(published by Rupa Publications)

The Bournvita Quiz Contest Quiz Book 2012
Bumper Bournvita Quiz Contest Quiz Book
Derek Introduces 100 Iconic Indians
Derek Introduces the Constitution and Parliament of India
Derek's Challenge
My Way: Success Mantras of 12 Achievers
Speak Up Speak Out
The Best of Bournvita Quiz Contest
The Bournvita Quiz Contest Quiz Book 2014
The Bournvita Quiz Contest Quiz Book 3
The Bournvita Quiz Contest Quiz Book 2017
The Essential BQC Quiz Book
The Ultimate Bournvita Quiz Contest Book of Knowledge Volume 1
The Ultimate Bournvita Quiz Contest Book of Knowledge Volume 2
The Ultimate Bournvita Quiz Contest Book of Knowledge Volume 3
The Ultimate Winning Minds Quiz Challenge
The School Quiz Book

THE GENERAL KNOWLEDGE QUIZ BOOK

DEREK O'BRIEN

RUPA

Published by
Rupa Publications India Pvt. Ltd 2018
7/16, Ansari Road, Daryaganj
New Delhi 110002

Sales Centres:
Allahabad Bengaluru Chennai
Hyderabad Jaipur Kathmandu
Kolkata Mumbai

Copyright © Derek O'Brien & Associates 2018

All rights reserved.
No part of this publication may be reproduced, stored in a retrieval system, or transmitted, in any form or by any means, electronic, mechanical, photocopying, recording or otherwise, without the prior permission of the publishers.

ISBN: 978-93-530-4025-3

First impression 2018

10 9 8 7 6 5 4 3 2 1

The moral right of the author has been asserted.

This book is sold subject to the condition that it shall not,
by way of trade or otherwise, be lent, resold, hired out, or otherwise
circulated, without the publisher's prior consent, in any form of
binding or cover other than that in which it is published.

CONTENTS

Animals in Fiction	1
Birds	4
Black	7
Brain	10
Cartoons and Comics	13
Clothes	16
Dance Forms	19
Days of the Week	22
Diseases and Disorders	25
Elections	28
Environment	31
Family Tree	34
Famous Addresses	37
Famous Detectives	40
Fashion	43
Festivals	46
Forts	49
Footwear	52
Gold	55
Harry Potter	58
History	61
Indian Railways	64
Indian Writers in English	67
Indoor Games	70
Insects	73
Inventions and Discoveries	76

Islands	79
Kings and Queens	82
Languages	85
Last Words	88
Light	91
Magical Numbers	94
Money	97
Music	100
National Flags	103
Nobel Prize	106
Oscars	109
Painters	112
Precious Stones	115
Science Fiction	118
Sequels and Prequels	121
Social Media	124
Sports in Films	127
Sweetmeats	130
Television	133
Tintin	136
US Presidents	139
Video Games	142
Wimbledon	145
Wonderful Words	148
Answers	151

ANIMALS IN FICTION

1. Which story relates the adventures of four animal friends and neighbours—Mole, Rat, Mr Toad of Toad Hall and Badger?
   a) *The Wind in the Willows*
   b) *The Jungle Book*
   c) *Black Beauty*

2. In Enid Blyton's Adventure Series, what was the name of Jack's intelligent and talkative parrot?
   a) Kiki
   b) Tim
   c) Winnie

3. The name Moby Dick was inspired by the name of a dangerous albino sperm whale. What was its called?
   a) Mocha Dick
   b) Mob Dick
   c) Maddison Dick

4. Which character in *Animal Farm* is directly modelled on the Soviet dictator Joseph Stalin?
   a) Boxer
   b) Napoleon
   c) Snowball

5. What kind of an animal is Rudyard Kipling's Rikki-Tikki-Tavi?

a) Gorilla
   b) Bear
   c) Mongoose

6. Which character created by Roald Dahl outwits the farmers Bean, Boggis and Bunce?
   a) Snowball
   b) King Louie
   c) Mr Fox

7. In the Harry Potter series, whose pet was Buckbeak, the Hippogriff?
   a) Albus Dumbledore
   b) Hagrid
   c) Draco Malfoy

8. Which of these is a story about Joe's prize collie and constant companion?
   a) *Ginger Pye*
   b) *Journey from Peppermint Street*
   c) *Lassie Come-Home*

9. In the famous novel by E.B. White, what is the name of the barn spider who manages to save Wilbur, the pig?
   a) Charlotte
   b) Stuart
   c) Nessie

10. Whom did T.S. Eliot call the 'Napoleon of Crime'?
    a) Heathcliff
    b) Macavity
    c) Snowbell

FUN TO KNOW

Walt Disney's cartoon dog Pluto was first named Rover. He became Pluto in the 1931 cartoon *The Moose Hunt*.

Winnie-the-Pooh got his first name from a brown bear that A.A. Milne's son saw in the London Zoo. The second name came from a swan the boy used to feed.

BIRDS

1. The bald eagle gets its name from 'balde' an old English word meaning...
   a) Graceful
   b) White
   c) Big

2. The bill of which of these birds is about a third of the length of its body and is serrated like a knife?
   a) Toco Toucan
   b) Roseate Spoonbill
   c) Crane

3. The Commonwealth Coat of Arms, the formal symbol of the Commonwealth of Australia, depicts a kangaroo and which bird?
   a) Peacock
   b) Emu
   c) Ostrich

4. The study or hobby of collecting birds' eggs is known as...
   a) Oology
   b) Epistemology
   c) Orology

5. Which bird lays the largest egg of any living bird in the world?

a) Eagle
   b) Ostrich
   c) Black Tern

6. Which of these birds is the national emblem of Guatemala and lends its name to its monetary unit?
   a) Resplendent Quetzal
   b) Kakapo
   c) Atlantic Puffin

7. 'Fled is that music:—Do I wake or sleep?', is the last line of which poem by John Keats?
   a) 'To a Waterfowl'
   b) 'Ode to a Nightingale'
   c) 'The Raven'

8. Which of the following terms would you use for a group of crows?
   a) Pandemonium
   b) Crime
   c) Murder

9. Which large South American bird shares its name with the second largest moon of Saturn?
   a) Greater Rhea
   b) Heron
   c) Grebe

10. Who directed the 1963 film *The Birds*?
    a) Robert Wise
    b) Alfred Hitchcock
    c) David Lean

FUN TO KNOW

The word 'sniper' originally came from India. It referred to a hunter who was skilled enough to shoot a species of wading birds called snipes.

A pelican's throat pouch can hold more water than its stomach.

BLACK

1. Which of the following terms means an unpredictable or unforeseen event, typically one with extreme consequences?
    a) Black Swan
    b) Black Bird
    c) Black Eagle

2. What is the colour of the hourglass-shaped mark found on the abdomens of female black widow spiders?
    a) Red
    b) Black
    c) Green

3. What is the process by which a black hole draws matter inward called?
    a) Acceleration
    b) Accretion
    c) Accentuation

4. Released on 25 July 1980, *Back in Black* was the seventh studio album of which Australian rock band?
    a) Bee Gees
    b) INXS
    c) AC/DC

5. In Marvel Comics, Black Panther protects the kingdom of…
   a) Sokovia
   b) Wakanda
   c) Halwan

6. In the novel, who among these was a friend of Black Beauty?
   a) Ginger
   b) Cardamom
   c) Clove

7. The 2005 film *Black* was based on which screenwriter's Gujarati play *Aatam Vinjhe Paankh*?
   a) Prakash Kapadia
   b) Anjum Rajabali
   c) Vishal Bhardwaj

8. In a game of snooker, how many points does a player get for potting the black ball?
   a) Five
   b) Seven
   c) Nine

9. Which of these is often referred to as black diamond?
   a) Coal
   b) Cobalt
   c) Pearl

10. In ancient Greek myths, initially the Black Sea was called Pontus Axeinus, which meant...
    a) Vast sea
    b) Inhospitable sea
    c) Calm sea

FUN TO KNOW

In January 1998, the New Zealand cricket team came to be known as the Black Caps after its sponsor, Clear Communications, held a competition to choose a name for the team.

The black forest cake gets its rich flavour and name from the liquor that comes from the variety of tart cherries grown in the Black Forest mountain region of Germany.

BRAIN

1. Which is the largest part of the human brain, accounting for 85 per cent of the organ's weight?
   a) Cerebellum
   b) Medulla Oblongata
   c) Cerebrum

2. According to popular belief, whose brain was stolen by Thomas Harvey from Princeton Hospital on 18 April 1955?
   a) Albert Einstein
   b) Pablo Picasso
   c) John F. Kennedy

3. Which animal has the largest brain of any creature on earth?
   a) Hippopotamus
   b) Sperm Whale
   c) African Elephant

4. Which bird is also called Brainfever bird as its call sounds like 'Brain Fever…Brain Fever'?
   a) Grey Francolin
   b) Common Hawk-Cuckoo
   c) Red-Wattled Lapwing

5. Dr Martin Philips is the protagonist of the novel *Brain*. Who is the author of the book?

a) Robin Cook
b) Michael Crichton
c) Arthur C. Clarke

6. Which term was coined by John McCarthy, an American computer scientist, in his proposal for the 1956 Dartmouth Conference which was the first conference devoted to the subject?
a) Artificial Intelligence
b) Gray matter
c) Short-term memory

7. The name of which of these comes from the Latin word for 'half skull'?
a) Migraine
b) Vertigo
c) Anaemia

8. In which film does Bradley Cooper take NZT, a drug that activates all the neurons in the brain?
a) *Limitless*
b) *Silver Linings Playbook*
c) *American Sniper*

9. According to Dr Frank Lynn Meshberger, *The Creation of Adam* allegorically portrays the moment when God bestowed Adam with intelligence. Who painted this famous work?
a) Michelangelo
b) Leonardo da Vinci
c) Rembrandt

10. Inflammation of the thin tissue that surrounds the brain and spinal cord is known as...
    a) Meningitis
    b) Cystitis
    c) Pleurisy

> **FUN TO KNOW**
>
> In 2000, black cab drivers in London were given brain scans by scientists at University College London. The test revealed that they had a much larger hippocampus compared with other people to accommodate their huge amount of navigating experience.
>
> In the human body, the left hemisphere controls the right half of the body, and vice versa.

CARTOONS AND COMICS

1. What were the original names given to the characters Tom and Jerry?
   a) Jasper and Jinx
   b) Pompom and Kiki
   c) Kitty and Tweety

2. During World War II, which cartoon character starred in the Academy Award-winning short film, *Der Fuehrer's Face*?
   a) Mickey Mouse
   b) Donald Duck
   c) Bugs Bunny

3. Stephen Hillenburg, a marine biologist, presented the idea of which show by placing a cartoon drawing of the lead character inside a fish tank?
   a) *The Octonauts*
   b) *The Deep*
   c) *SpongeBob SquarePants*

4. In which of these towns is *The Flintstones* set?
   a) Bedrock
   b) Riverdale
   c) Wessex

5. The name of which of these characters was taken from a line in Frank Sinatra's 'Strangers in the Night'?

a) Scooby-Doo
   b) Boo-Boo Bear
   c) Foghorn Leghorn

6. In 1997, who became the first cartoon character to appear on a postage stamp in the US?
   a) Bugs Bunny
   b) Road Runner
   c) Mickey Mouse

7. Who is the famous son of Poopdeck Pappy?
   a) Porky Pig
   b) Popeye
   c) Daffy Duck

8. Which cartoon series is adapted from the classic comic strip *Lot Pot*?
   a) Motu Patlu
   b) Chhota Bheem
   c) Mighty Raju

9. What breed of dog is Charlie Brown's Snoopy?
   a) Great Dane
   b) Beagle
   c) Fox Terrier

10. The main characters of which comic strip are named after a sixteenth-century theologian and a seventeenth-century English philosopher?
    a) *Peanuts*
    b) *Calvin and Hobbes*
    c) *Tintin*

FUN TO KNOW

A real life one-eyed sailor from Chester, Illinois, named Frank 'Rocky' Fiegal, who had a fondness for fighting and pipe-smoking, was the inspiration for Popeye.

The film, *Who Framed Roger Rabbit*, was the only time when Disney's Mickey Mouse and Warner Bros' Bugs Bunny were seen together on screen.

CLOTHES

1. Which of these is named after James Thomas Brudenell, who led the charge of the Light Brigade, and whose troops first wore such garments?
   a) Mackintosh
   b) Sweater
   c) Cardigan

2. Which of these words, of Scandinavian origin, was used as a verb in Middle English to mean 'tuck up around the body'?
   a) Poncho
   b) Kilt
   c) Kimono

3. In which country did the Panama hat originate?
   a) Chile
   b) Ecuador
   c) Panama

4. Dirndl, puffball and pencil are different types of...
   a) Trousers
   b) Hats
   c) Skirts

5. Who among these would normally wear a tutu?
   a) A female ballet dancer
   b) A female gymnast

c) A female swimmer

6. Which of these is a pair of knee-length trousers, cut with full legs to resemble a skirt?
   a) Culottes
   b) Jeggings
   c) Anoraks

7. What does a grabatologist collect?
   a) Coats
   b) Ties
   c) Socks

8. In which country would you come across a girl wearing a sarafan, a long-sleeved peasant blouse, and an ornate kokoshnik?
   a) Japan
   b) Russia
   c) France

9. Tuxedo is said to have been first worn in the millionaire district of Tuxedo Park in...
   a) USA
   b) UK
   c) Australia

10. The trilby hat is named after the heroine of the novel *Trilby* by...
    a) George du Maurier
    b) Truman Capote
    c) G.B. Shaw

FUN TO KNOW

The four pockets on the jacket of the Mao suit were said to signify the Four Cardinal Principles in the Chinese classic *I Ching*: propriety, justice, honesty, and a sense of shame.

During World War II, Oliver Lyttelton, President of the Board of Trade of Great Britain introduced clothes rationing.

DANCE FORMS

1. Which dance form was introduced in the fifteenth century AD by the Vaishnava saint of Assam, Mahapurusha Sankaradeva?
   a) Sattriya
   b) Kathakali
   c) Manipuri

2. Complete the following idiom with the name of a dance form: It takes two to_____.
   a) Samba
   b) Salsa
   c) Tango

3. Which of these forms of music and dance is associated with the Roma people of the Andalusia region of southern Spain?
   a) Kabuki
   b) Flamenco
   c) Samba

4. The Rasleela dances of which state originated during the reign of King Bhagyachandra in the eighteenth century?
   a) Uttar Pradesh
   b) Manipur
   c) West Bengal

5. The name of which dance form comes from the German word for 'revolve'?
   a) Waltz
   b) Ballet
   c) Rumba

6. Which dance form derives its textual sanction from *Balarama Bharatam* and *Hastalakshana Deepika*?
   a) Kathakali
   b) Odissi
   c) Manipuri

7. In the 1920s, who danced with Anna Pavlova and created the dance 'A Hindu Wedding'?
   a) Uday Shankar
   b) Birju Maharaj
   c) Lachchu Maharaj

8. The three distinct styles of which dance form are from the regions of Seraikella, Purulia and Mayurbhanj?
   a) Bihu
   b) Chhau
   c) Dollu Kunitha

9. Which word connects a Spanish dance in simple triple time and a woman's short open jacket?
   a) Fox-trot
   b) Bolero
   c) Cha Cha Cha

10. According to belief, Tarantella, a folk dance form of Italy, was performed to cure the victim from the bite of a species of...
    a) Scorpion
    b) Dog
    c) Spider

FUN TO KNOW

Bharatanatyam was originally known as Sadhir. It owes its present name to E. Krishna Iyer and Rukmini Devi Arundale.

Rouf is a famous dance form of Jammu and Kashmir that welcomes the spring season.

DAYS OF THE WEEK

1. Though the term 'Black Friday' is now associated with shopping, it was first used to describe which event?
    a) Pearl Harbour attack
    b) Crash of the US gold market
    c) Assassination of John F. Kennedy

2. Which is the only day in the English language named after a Roman god?
    a) Tuesday
    b) Saturday
    c) Thursday

3. What is the name of the character who becomes Robinson Crusoe's servant?
    a) Monday
    b) Wednesday
    c) Friday

4. In which 1982 film would you come across characters named Shani, Shom and Budh?
    a) *Saat Hindustani*
    b) *Jo Jeeta Wohi Sikandar*
    c) *Satte Pe Satta*

5. What does 'Mardi Gras' literally mean in French?
    a) Mad Monday

b) Fat Tuesday
c) Fun Thursday

6. Which of these is a popular song from the John Badham directed *Saturday Night Fever*?
   a) Streets of Philadelphia
   b) Stayin' Alive
   c) Take My Breath Away

7. Which day of the week does Garfield hate the most?
   a) Saturday
   b) Sunday
   c) Monday

8. Who, according to a rhyme, 'married on Wednesday' but 'took ill on Thursday'?
   a) Tristan Shandy
   b) Solomon Grundy
   c) Little Bo Beep

9. Which Roman Emperor adopted the seven-day week in AD 321 and made Sunday a day of rest?
   a) Caligula
   b) Constantine
   c) Julius Caesar

10. According to the Christian calendar, which day of the week marks the start of Lent?
    a) Wednesday
    b) Sunday
    c) Friday

FUN TO KNOW

The story of the Naseeruddin Shah starrer *A Wednesday!* revolves around a fateful Wednesday between 2 p.m. and 6 p.m. This film was officially remade into a Hollywood film *A Common Man* starring Ben Kingsley.

Bob Geldof's song 'I Don't Like Mondays' was written after he read about a woman going on a shooting spree because she did not like Mondays.

DISEASES AND DISORDERS

1. Which of these diseases gets its name from a word in the Kimakonde language, meaning 'to become contorted'?
   a) Zika
   b) Dengue
   c) Chikungunya

2. What is believed to have been developed by Felix Hoffmann in order to help his rheumatic father?
   a) Aspirin
   b) Insulin
   c) Penicillin

3. Which of these is an eating disorder that causes people to lose more weight than is considered healthy for their age and height?
   a) Autism
   b) Anorexia
   c) Schizophrenia

4. Shah Rukh Khan suffered from which disorder in the film *My Name is Khan*?
   a) Barlow Syndrome
   b) Down syndrome
   c) Asperger's Syndrome

5. Hepatitis B is a potentially life-threatening infection of the...
   a) Pharynx
   b) Liver
   c) Heart

6. Which of these is a blood-related genetic disorder?
   a) Anthrax
   b) Filariasis
   c) Thalassaemia

7. With the treatment of which disease are Sarah Nelmes and James Phipps associated?
   a) Measles
   b) Small pox
   c) Cholera

8. In 1947, which virus was first identified in monkeys in Uganda?
   a) HIV
   b) Ebola
   c) Zika

9. In 1923, Frederick G. Banting and John Macleod received the Nobel Prize in Physiology or Medicine for the discovery of...
   a) Insulin
   b) Penicillin
   c) Smallpox vaccine

10. In 1795, the Admiralty made the issue of lemon juice compulsory on ships to counter which disease?
    a) Scurvy
    b) Asthma
    c) Cholera

> **FUN TO KNOW**
>
> In 2014, the World Health Organization (WHO) declared India polio-free and in 2016, India was acknowledged as the first country in the world to be declared free of a disease called yaws.
>
> After falling while ice skating during his first year at Cambridge University, brilliant theoretical physicist Stephen Hawking was told he had the degenerative motor neuron disease, Amyotrophic Lateral Sclerosis (ALS) and had only two and a half years to live.

ELECTIONS

1. In 1949, Golda Meir was elected to the Knesset, which is the parliament of…
   a) Israel
   b) Russia
   c) Germany

2. Which actor defeated Hemvati Nandan Bahuguna in the 1984 General Elections?
   a) Shatrughan Sinha
   b) Amitabh Bachchan
   c) Vinod Khanna

3. Which of these words originally denoted a small coloured ball placed in a container to register a vote?
   a) Franchise
   b) Suffrage
   c) Ballot

4. In 1982, the Electronic Voting Machine was used for the first time in the Assembly Election of which State?
   a) Kerala
   b) West Bengal
   c) Rajasthan

5. How do voters in Gambia vote?
   a) Placing flags in front of the pictures of the candidates

b) Throwing darts on the pictures of candidates
   c) Dropping marbles into bins that have the candidate's picture on them

6. In 1872, Victoria Woodhull became the first woman to run for President of…
   a) New Zealand
   b) USA
   c) Germany

7. Who appoints the Chief Election Commissioner of India?
   a) Prime Minister of India
   b) President of India
   c) Chief Justice of Supreme Court

8. In which country were mock elections held on 21 April 2007 to prepare the people for the change to democracy?
   a) Thailand
   b) Bhutan
   c) Burma

9. Which was the first self-governing country in the world to grant all women the right to vote in parliamentary elections?
   a) Mexico
   b) New Zealand
   c) USA

10. Who played the role of Tracy Enid Flick in the 1999 film *Election*?
    a) Reese Witherspoon
    b) Renée Zellweger
    c) Kate Winslet

FUN TO KNOW

Since 1997, astronauts on the International Space Station have been able to vote in elections in the US.

People aged 16–18 can vote in Bosnia, Serbia and Montenegro but only if they are employed.

ENVIRONMENT

1. Which of these terms was coined by Ernst Haeckel?
   a) Biome
   b) Acid Rain
   c) Ecology

2. Which former Vice President of the US jointly received the Nobel Peace Prize in 2007 for his work on climate change?
   a) Al Gore
   b) George W. Bush
   c) Joe Biden

3. Name the movement started in the 1970s by the mountain women of North India who hugged trees to save them from being cut down.
   a) Humsafar Movement
   b) Chipko Movement
   c) Rakshak Movement

4. In 1984, toxic methyl isocyanate gas leaked from a pesticide factory in which city in India?
   a) Jaipur
   b) Kochi
   c) Bhopal

5. Jane Goodall is renowned for her long-term research on which animal at the Gombe Stream National Park in Tanzania?

a) Crocodile
b) Chimpanzee
c) Elephant

6. In which film does Julia Roberts become a legal assistant and bring down a California power company accused of polluting a city's water supply?
   a) *Eat Pray Love*
   b) *Notting Hill*
   c) *Erin Brockovich*

7. In 1971, which organization was founded to oppose US nuclear testing at Amchitka Island?
   a) Amnesty International
   b) Greenpeace
   c) Friends of Nature

8. In 1985, a group of scientists published the first paper on losses of ozone over which region?
   a) North Pole
   b) Mariana Trench
   c) Antarctica

9. Which film, set in 2805, is about a robot who needs to clean up the garbage on Earth?
   a) *WALL-E*
   b) *Inside Out*
   c) *Big Hero 6*

10. Which Nobel laureate founded the Green Belt Movement, an environmental non-governmental organization?
    a) Wangari Maathai
    b) Joy Adamson
    c) Ellen Johnson Sirleaf

> **FUN TO KNOW**
>
> The UN celebrates World Environment Day on 5 June every year.
>
> Recycling one aluminum can can save enough energy to run a TV for three hours.

FAMILY TREE

1. Who among these was the older brother of the legendary cartoonist, R.K. Laxman?
   a) Mulk Raj Anand
   b) R.K. Narayan
   c) Raja Rao

2. Which Mughal emperor was the father of Jahanara Begum?
   a) Akbar
   b) Shah Jahan
   c) Aurangzeb

3. Name the musical band that was formed by Michael Jackson and his brothers?
   a) Jackson and His Brothers
   b) Jackson 5
   c) Jackson's Family

4. Who is the famous mother of Saif Ali Khan?
   a) Hema Malini
   b) Sharmila Tagore
   c) Dimple Kapadia

5. Who succeeded his father-in-law, Gardiner Hubbard, as president of the National Geographic Society between 1898 and 1903?
   a) Alexander Graham Bell

b) Thomas Alva Edison
c) Humphry Davy

6. Karan Johar's mother Hiroo is Yash Chopra's...
   a) Aunt
   b) Sister
   c) Daughter

7. According to *The Mysterious Island*, Captain Nemo is a descendant of ...
   a) Tipu Sultan
   b) Prithiviraj Chauhan
   c) Babur

8. Milkha Singh's son Jeev Milkha Singh is associated with which sport?
   a) Boxing
   b) Golf
   c) Archery

9. In 1915, which scientist shared the Nobel Prize for Physics with his son?
   a) William Henry Bragg
   b) Jan Tinbergen
   c) Niels Bohr

10. Tippi Hedren, the star of Alfred Hitchcock's *The Birds*, is the grandmother of...
    a) Dakota Johnson
    b) Anne Hathaway
    c) Mila Kunis

FUN TO KNOW

In 2013, daughters Anoushka Shankar and Norah Jones accepted the Lifetime Achievement Grammy Award on behalf of their father Pandit Ravi Shankar.

Simpsons creator Matt Groening named his cartoon family after members of his own. Matt's grandfather Abram Groening shares his name with Grandpa Abe.

FAMOUS ADDRESSES

1. 1600 Pennsylvania Avenue NW, Washington, DC 20500 is the address of the...
   a) White House
   b) United Nations Headquarters
   c) Empire State Building

2. The Anne Frank House is located at Prinsengracht 263–267 in...
   a) Amsterdam
   b) Paris
   c) Berlin

3. In which of these stories do Sherlock Holmes and John Watson begin their tenancy at 221B Baker Street?
   a) *The Hound of the Baskervilles*
   b) *The Sign of Four*
   c) *A Study in Scarlet*

4. In 1941, who escaped from the house at 38/2, Lala Lajpat Rai Sarani, Kolkata-700 020?
   a) Subhas Chandra Bose
   b) Aurobindo Ghosh
   c) Bipin Chandra Pal

5. Who has the name 'Sanders' written over the door of his house?

a) Mickey Mouse
   b) Yogi Bear
   c) Winnie-the-Pooh

6. Who is the famous occupant of 124 Conch Street, Bikini Bottom, Pacific Ocean?
   a) Captain Nemo
   b) SpongeBob SquarePants
   c) Moby Dick

7. If you are at 405 East 42nd Street, New York, NY, 10017, USA, where would you be?
   a) Empire State Building
   b) United States Capitol
   c) United Nations Headquarters

8. The last private resident of which landmark was called Mr Chicken?
   a) 10, Downing Steet, London
   b) White House
   c) Rashtrapati Bhawan

9. Who coined the name 'Invention Factory' for his research and development facility at Menlo Park?
   a) Alexander Graham Bell
   b) Thomas Alva Edison
   c) J.L. Baird

10. Whose address is North Pole, HOH OHO, Canada?
    a) Snow Queen
    b) Robin Hood
    c) Santa Claus

FUN TO KNOW

In India, Postal Index Number (PIN) is a 6-digit code. The first digit indicates one of the 9 PIN regions in the country. While the first 8 are geographical regions, the digit 9 is reserved for the Army Postal Service.

Anand Bhavan is a famous landmark in Allahabad. It was the ancestral home of the Nehru family. It has now been turned into a museum.

FAMOUS DETECTIVES

1. Who among these detectives was created by Agatha Christie?
   a) Harley Quin
   b) Marcus Didius Falco
   c) Inspector Endeavour Morse

2. Who purchased his Stradivarius from a Jew broker in London's Tottenham Court Road, for 55 shillings?
   a) Sherlock Holmes
   b) Hercule Poirot
   c) Miss Marple

3. Which young detective has a housekeeper named Hannah Gruen?
   a) Veronica Mars
   b) Miss Marple
   c) Nancy Drew

4. Rajani Sen Road, Ballygunge, Kolkata is the address of which famous detective?
   a) Byomkesh Bakshi
   b) Feluda
   c) Kakababu

5. Which fictional detective was modelled on François-Eugène Vidocq, one-time criminal and founder of the French police detective organization Sûreté?

a) Harley Quin
b) C. Auguste Dupin
c) Ariadne Oliver

6. Which fictional detective featured in Raymond Chandler's novels *The Long Goodbye, The Lady in the Lake* and *The Big Sleep*?
   a) Kinsey Millhone
   b) Philip Marlowe
   c) Phryne Fisher

7. Which famous author created the priest-detective Father Brown?
   a) G.K. Chesterton
   b) G.B. Shaw
   c) P.G. Wodehouse

8. Who was the first fictional character to receive an obituary on the front of *The New York Times*?
   a) Sherlock Holmes
   b) Hercule Poirot
   c) Miss Marple

9. Which of these characters was created by Frederic Dannay and Manfred B. Lee?
   a) Philo Vance
   b) Peter Wimsey
   c) Ellery Queen

10. In which novel by Agatha Christie does Miss Marple make her first appearance?
    a) *The Murder at the Vicarage*
    b) *A Murder is Announced*
    c) *The Mirror Crack'd from Side to Side*

> **FUN TO KNOW**
>
> Edgar Allen Poe's story, 'The Murders in the Rue Morgue', is generally considered to be the first detective story.
>
> J.K. Rowling adopted the pseudonym Robert Galbraith to write the detective novels *Career of Evil, Silkworm* and *The Cuckoo's Calling*. She chose the name Robert Galbraith by merging the name of her political hero Robert F. Kennedy and her childhood fantasy name Ella Galbraith.

FASHION

1. Which fashion designer was credited with the creation of the Little Black Dress in 1926?
   a) Coco Chanel
   b) John Galliano
   c) Donatella Versace

2. Which famous fashion model wrote the book *Swan*?
   a) Kate Moss
   b) Naomi Campbell
   c) Tyra Banks

3. Who designed Audrey Hepburn's first Oscar dress as well as the famous black satin gown she wore in the film *Breakfast at Tiffany's*?
   a) Hubert de Givenchy
   b) Coco Chanel
   c) Christian Dior

4. Bhanu Athaiya shared an Oscar with John Mollo for designing the costumes for which film?
   a) *East Is East*
   b) *Gandhi*
   c) *Life of Pi*

5. Complete the lyrics of the song 'Rainbow High' sung by Madonna: 'I came from the people, they need to adore me/So _____ me from my head to my toes…'

a) Christian Dior
b) Versace
c) Gucci

6. He was the first Indian designer to showcase his collection at the Paris Fashion Week. He collaborated with Reebok and designed a sportswear line called Fish Fry. He was also appointed the Creative Director of the Spanish fashion brand Paco Robanne. Name him.
   a) Sandeep Khosla
   b) Manish Arora
   c) Sabyasachi Mukherjee

7. By increasing the height of heels from 6 cm to 8 cm, Roger Vivier invented which of these?
   a) Wedge heels
   b) Kitten heels
   c) Aiguille stiletto

8. This saree is a Geographical Indication tagged product of Tamil Nadu. The main technique of weaving this saree is called Korvai. Identify the sari.
   a) Kanjeevaram
   b) Paithani
   c) Tangail

9. Who created the famous reality TV series *America's Next Top Model*?
   a) Gisele Bündchen
   b) Naomi Campbell
   c) Tyra Banks

10. The film *The Devil Wears Prada* is based on the book written by Lauren Weisberger, who is said to have written it based on her experience as whose assistant?
    a) Laura Brown
    b) Emmanuelle Alt
    c) Anna Wintour

FUN TO KNOW

In the TV series *Friends*, the character played by Jennifer Aniston used to work for the designer Ralph Lauren, who also made a guest appearance on the show.

The Nehru jacket, the hip-length tailored coat named after Jawaharlal Nehru, was also popular with the Beatles. In 2013, John Lennon's teal blue jacket was sold for £7,000.

FESTIVALS

1. Which unique festival is held in the little town of Buñol, near Valencia, each August?
   a) La Tomatina
   b) Vendimia
   c) Olivagando

2. In which state is Shigmo Utsav celebrated?
   a) Goa
   b) Jammu and Kashmir
   c) Gujarat

3. Since 1989, which city has hosted the International Kite Festival as part of the official celebration of Uttarayan?
   a) Trivandrum
   b) Nagpur
   c) Ahmedabad

4. The name of which festival comes from Sanskrit words meaning 'astrological passage'?
   a) Rosh Hashanah
   b) Songkran
   c) Yom Kippur

5. Barsana village in Uttar Pradesh is famous for...
   a) Thai Pongal
   b) Hornbill Festival

c) Lathmar Holi

6. Which festival is also known as 'the Day of Remembrance' as the Jews commemorate the creation of the world on this day?
   a) Rosh Hashanah
   b) Sadeh
   c) Qingming

7. The Lantern Festival in China and other Asian countries honours...
   a) The Hwang Ho
   b) The Sun God
   c) Deceased ancestors

8. In which festival in Bihar is the rising and setting sun worshipped?
   a) Chhath
   b) Bihu
   c) Rath Yatra

9. Which of these is an important Theravada Buddhist festival, commemorating the birth, enlightenment, and death of the Buddha?
   a) Koningsdag
   b) Hanukkah
   c) Wesak

10. Which author wrote about the Kumbh Mela: 'It is wonderful, the power of a faith like that, that can make multitudes upon multitudes of the old

and weak and the young and frail enter without hesitation...marvelous to our kind of people, the cold whites'?
a) Rudyard Kipling
b) Mark Twain
c) Charles Dickens

FUN TO KNOW

Sukkot celebrates Israel's bountiful harvests and recalls the time when the Israelites wandered the desert living in temporary shelters.

Armenians celebrate Christmas on 6 January. This was the original date for the celebration of the birth of Jesus until the fourth century when it was changed to 25 December by the Roman Catholic Church.

FORTS

1. In which fort was Nazam, a water-carrier, who had saved Humayun from drowning, crowned emperor for half a day?
   a) Purana Qila
   b) Red Fort
   c) Agra Fort

2. The Hayat-Bakhsh-bagh, Nahr-i-Bihisht, marble pavilions Sawan and Bhadon are parts of which complex?
   a) Red Fort
   b) Mehrangarh Fort
   c) Sinhagad

3. Which of these forts gets its name from a Telugu word meaning Shepherd's Hill?
   a) Chittorgarh Fort
   b) Golconda Fort
   c) Jaisalmer Fort

4. Who was imprisoned in Qila Mubarak in Bathinda after being defeated by Malik Altunia?
   a) Nur Jehan
   b) Rani Lakshmibai
   c) Razia Sultan

5. The Sher Mandal, found in the Purana Qila, is

believed to have been used by which emperor as his library?
a) Ashoka
b) Humayun
c) Tipu Sultan

6. The building of the Cuttack Railway Station in Odisha was inspired by which of these forts?
a) Barabati Fort
b) Shivneri Fort
c) Munger Fort

7. Which fort was described by Babur as 'the pearl amongst the fortresses of Hind'?
a) Warangal Fort
b) The Gwalior Fort
c) Sindhudurg Fort

8. The capital of which state gets its name from the Ita Fort?
a) Andhra Pradesh
b) Himachal Pradesh
c) Arunachal Pradesh

9. Shivaji was born in which of these forts?
a) Shivneri
b) Ahmadnagar
c) Janjira

10. Which fort was built by Raja Bir Singh Deo in 1613 on the hill known as Bangara?
    a) Bidar Fort
    b) Gulbarga Fort
    c) Jhansi Fort

FUN TO KNOW

Ala-ud-din Khilji is said to have been so enamoured by Queen Padmini that he attacked the Chittorgarh Fort in 1303 to abduct her.

In 2013, six hill forts in Rajasthan—Amber, Chittorgarh, Gangron, Jaisalmer, Kumbhalgarh and Ranthambhore—were added to the list of UNESCO World Heritage Sites.

FOOTWEAR

1. To symbolize their superiority over comic actors, the tragic actors of ancient Greek plays wore 'Buskins'. These were a type of...
   a) Closed-toe sandals
   b) Pointed-heeled shoes
   c) Raised platform shoes

2. Which of these is defined by the Oxford Dictionary as 'a strong outdoor shoe with ornamental perforated patterns in the leather'?
   a) Brogue
   b) Penny Loafer
   c) Slip-ons

3. Which shoe gets its name from a character from the Buster Brown comic strip which first appeared in the *New York Herald* in 1902?
   a) Mary Jane shoe
   b) Blucher shoe
   c) Dori shoes

4. Which of these shoes are also known as Saleem Shahis as they were popularized by the Mughal king Saleem Shah?
   a) Khapusa
   b) Mojaris
   c) Padukas

5. What is the metal or plastic tube fixed around each end of a shoelace called?
    a) Shank
    b) Vamp
    c) Aglet

6. Which of the following is a woman's slipper or light shoe without a back and derives its name from the French word for slipper?
    a) Stiletto
    b) Mule
    c) Espadrille

7. Which of these is a foot-measuring device you would find in a footwear store?
    a) Beaufort Device
    b) Snellen's Device
    c) Brannock Device

8. Which of these is a knee-length waterproof rubber or plastic boot?
    a) Espadrilles
    b) Wellington
    c) Slingbacks

9. Who wrote the novel *One Two Buckle My Shoe* featuring a pair of brand new patent leather shoes with large gleaming buckles?
    a) Agatha Christie
    b) J.K. Rowling
    c) Charles Dickens

10. Which shoe shares its name with a city in central England, on the river Thames, a town in north central Mississippi, and a heavy cotton cloth chiefly used to make shirts?
    a) Boot
    b) Brogue
    c) Oxford

> **FUN TO KNOW**
>
> Men were the first to wear heels as those of them who rode horses needed their boots to have heels in order to stay in their stirrups.
>
> Salvatore Ferragamo invented the wedge shoe when Italy was suffering from closed trade with other countries in the 1940s as he could no longer purchase steel for his traditional heels.

GOLD

1. In the film *Goldfinger*, James Bond uncovers a plot to contaminate a gold reserve named...
   a) Fort Brigade
   b) Fort Knox
   c) Fort Kuber

2. The Golden Temple in Amritsar was designed by...
   a) Guru Arjan Dev
   b) Guru Nanak
   c) Guru Gobind Singh

3. The endangered Golden Lion Tamarin, found in the forests of Rio de Janeiro, is a type of...
   a) Primate
   b) Rodent
   c) Insect

4. Which word, introduced by Sher Shah Suri, was used for a gold coin weighing 169 grains?
   a) Dam
   b) Rupiya
   c) Mohur

5. In 1581, who was knighted aboard the *Golden Hind*?
   a) Christopher Columbus
   b) James Cook
   c) Sir Francis Drake

6. Which mineral is also called 'fool's gold' because of its physical resemblance with gold?
   a) Bentonite
   b) Alunite
   c) Pyrite

7. The Golden Chariot Train is a joint venture of the Ministry of Railways and the State government of...
   a) Kerala
   b) Karnataka
   c) Rajasthan

8. Who won the Sahitya Akademi Award for *The Golden Gate*?
   a) Vikram Seth
   b) Anita Desai
   c) Mulk Raj Anand

9. Who rid himself of his golden touch by bathing in the Pactolus River?
   a) Tutankhamen
   b) Midas
   c) Thor

10. If the first major 'gold rush' took place in North America, where did the second one begin in 1851?
    a) Australia
    b) India
    c) South Africa

FUN TO KNOW

India won its first Olympic gold in 1928 in field hockey and in 2008, Abhinav Bindra became the first Indian to win an individual gold medal at the Olympic Games.

The 1925 film *The Gold Rush* was directed by Charles Chaplin and was nominated for two Oscars.

HARRY POTTER

1. At Hogwarts, Gilderoy Lockhart, Sybill Trelawney and Garrick Ollivander belonged to...
   a) Hufflepuff House
   b) Ravenclaw House
   c) Gryffindor House

2. Which ingredient of polyjuice potion must be picked during a full moon?
   a) Knotgrass
   b) Lacewing flies
   c) Fluxweed

3. In the Diagon Alley, what did Flourish and Blotts sell?
   a) Books
   b) Robes
   c) Wands

4. In a game of Quidditch, each team has a Keeper, a Seeker, three Chasers and two...
   a) Catchers
   b) Beaters
   c) Slappers

5. 'One simply siphons the excess thoughts from one's mind, pours them into the basin, and examines them at one's leisure.' Which basin was Dumbledore talking about?

a) Basilisk
b) Pensieve
c) Horcrux

6. Named after Severus Snape, *Harryplax severus* is a species of...
   a) Jellyfish
   b) Crab
   c) Dinosaur

7. There were four creators and contributors to the Marauder's Map. If James Potter, Sirius Black and Remus Lupin were three, who was the fourth?
   a) Severus Snape
   b) Peter Pettigrew
   c) Rowena Ravenclaw

8. What was the name of the goblin who escorted Harry Potter to his vault on his first ever trip to Gringotts bank?
   a) Griphook
   b) Dobby
   c) Hippogriff

9. During the Triwizard Tournament, Harry Potter had to steal a golden egg from which of these dragons?
   a) Welsh Green
   b) Swedish Short-Snout
   c) Hungarian Horntail

10. What is the incantation for the Summoning Charm?
    a) Incendio
    b) Revelio
    c) Accio

FUN TO KNOW

Hogwarts Headache is a generalized headache that a person gets after spending many hours reading an unusually long book such as a Harry Potter book. The term was coined by Dr Howard J. Bennett in a Letter to the Editor of *The New England Journal of Medicine* on 30 October 2003.

The drafts of *Harry Potter and the Deathly Hallows* were code named *Edinburgh Potters* and *The Life and Times of Clara Rose Lovett* to prevent them from leaking.

HISTORY

1. The assassination of Archduke Franz Ferdinand was one of the major reasons that led to...
   a) Crimean War
   b) World War I
   c) World War II

2. After seizing political power in 1799, which military leader crowned himself emperor in 1804?
   a) Arthur Wellesley, 1st Duke of Wellington
   b) Napoleon Bonaparte
   c) Horatio Nelson, 1st Viscount Nelson

3. What does the word 'Renaissance' mean in French?
   a) Renunciation
   b) Rebirth
   c) Restoration

4. What was the pseudonym of François-Marie Arouet?
   a) Rousseau
   b) Voltaire
   c) Aristotle

5. Who delivered the famous 'Blood, toil, tears and sweat' speech?
   a) Abraham Lincoln
   b) John F. Kennedy
   c) Winston Churchill

6. Which famous battle was fought by the Bhaghirathi River?
   a) Battle of Buxar
   b) Battle of Plassey
   c) Third Battle of Panipat

7. The Apollo 11 mission occurred eight years after who announced a national goal of landing a man on the moon by the end of the 1960s?
   a) John F. Kennedy
   b) Jimmy Carter
   c) Ronald Reagan

8. The Terracotta Army is a part of a mausoleum of the first emperor of…
   a) Burma
   b) Vietnam
   c) China

9. When President Franklin D. Roosevelt said, 'A date which will live in infamy', what was he referring to?
   a) Boston Tea Party
   b) Attack on Pearl Harbor
   c) Assassination of Abraham Lincoln

10. Simon Bolivar was the dictator of which country from 1823 to 1826?
    a) Bolivia
    b) Peru
    c) Uruguay

FUN TO KNOW

The reunification of East and West Germany was made official on 3 October 1990, almost one year after the fall of the Berlin Wall.

On 14 May 1948, the day on which the British Mandate over Palestine expired, Jewish Agency Chairman David Ben-Gurion proclaimed the State of Israel. The new State was recognized the same night by the United States and three days later by the USSR.

INDIAN RAILWAYS

1. In which present-day state did the Kakori Train Robbery take place?
   a) Maharashtra
   b) Uttar Pradesh
   c) Odisha

2. In 2008, the Maitree Express was launched to connect India to which country?
   a) Pakistan
   b) Nepal
   c) Bangladesh

3. After which author's work is the Godan Express named?
   a) Valmiki
   b) Munshi Premchand
   c) Kalidasa

4. Which special train was launched to mark the 100th birth anniversary of Agnes Gonxha Bojaxhiu?
   a) Mother Express
   b) Ahimsa Express
   c) Shanti Express

5. On 12 February 1948, whose ashes were carried to Triveni in a third-class compartment numbered 2949?
   a) Mahatma Gandhi

b) Jawaharlal Nehru
c) Lal Bahadur Shastri

6. Ghum, the highest railway station in India, is located in which state?
   a) West Bengal
   b) Himachal Pradesh
   c) Tamil Nadu

7. Which of these trains has restaurants named Maharaja and Maharani?
   a) Palace on Wheels
   b) Golden Chariot
   c) The Deccan Odyssey

8. Which is the oldest surviving functional steam engine in the world?
   a) Fairy Queen
   b) Queen Victoria
   c) Deccan Odyssey

9. The Chetak Express runs between Delhi and which of these cities?
   a) Simla
   b) Udaipur
   c) Mumbai

10. Who is the author of the book *The Great Railway Bazaar*?
    a) Paul Theroux
    b) Rudyard Kipling
    c) Ruskin Bond

FUN TO KNOW

Mahendra Singh Dhoni was once a ticket collector at Kharagpur station. He was rejected by the Railways cricket team in 2002 because the selectors did not find him technically sound.

The first train in India ran from Bombay to Thane for around 34 kilometres on 16 April 1853. There was a 21-gun salute when the train was flagged off.

INDIAN WRITERS IN ENGLISH

1. Who once asked his friend Purna to weigh the manuscript of his first book with 'a stone and drown it in the Thames' if he could not find a publisher?
   a) R.K. Narayan
   b) Mulk Raj Anand
   c) Raja Rao

2. Who co-authored the screenplay of the Salman Khan-starrer *Kick*?
   a) Amitav Ghosh
   b) Amish Tripathi
   c) Chetan Bhagat

3. Who wrote the preface to Mulk Raj Anand's *Untouchable*?
   a) Rudyard Kipling
   b) E.M. Forster
   c) T.S. Eliot

4. Her first novel won her the Man Booker Prize. Her second novel, published after nineteen years, made it to the longlist of the Man Booker Prize. Name her.
   a) Kiran Desai
   b) Anita Desai
   c) Arundhati Roy

5. Which is the final book in the Ibis Trilogy?

a) *Flood of Fire*
   b) *Sea of Poppies*
   c) *River of Smoke*

6. In which book does Balram Halwai narrate his story through letters he writes, but doesn't send, to the Chinese premier, Wen Jiabao?
   a) *The Hungry Tide*
   b) *The White Tiger*
   c) *English, August*

7. Which of these works by Vikram Seth is based on Charles Johnston's translation of Aleksandr Pushkin's novel in verse *Eugene Onegin*?
   a) *From Heaven Lake*
   b) *A Suitable Boy*
   c) *The Golden Gate*

8. *Lone Fox Dancing* is the autobiography of which author?
   a) Ruskin Bond
   b) Nayantara Sahgal
   c) Amitav Ghosh

9. Which famous author and poet was married to actress Leela Naidu?
   a) Dom Moraes
   b) Nirad C. Chaudhuri
   c) Nissim Ezekiel

10. Who won the Sahitya Akademi Award in 2002 for the novel *A New World*?
    a) Amit Chaudhuri
    b) Amitav Ghosh
    c) Vikram Seth

FUN TO KNOW

The manuscript of *The Immortals of Meluha* was rejected by twenty-odd publishers because they thought it was a religious book and would not interest the youth of today. Finally, the author Amish Tripathi self-published it.

Anita Desai was the first woman to win the Sahitya Akademi Award for a work in the English language. She received it in 1978 for her novel *Fire on the Mountain*.

INDOOR GAMES

1. How many balls are used in a game of snooker?
   a) 22
   b) 20
   c) 15

2. Which sport made its Olympic debut in 1992 in Barcelona?
   a) Badminton
   b) Boxing
   c) Archery

3. After 1475, the chess piece that used to be then called the counselor gained increased mobility and became the piece which we now call the...
   a) Bishop
   b) Queen
   c) Rook

4. In the game of bowling, when a bowler achieves three strikes in a row, what is it called?
   a) Chicken
   b) Turkey
   c) Eagle

5. In which country did Mah-Jong originate?
   a) Japan
   b) China

c) India

6. With which sport would you associate the flutter kick, the dolphin kick and the scissors kick?
   a) Swimming
   b) Karate
   c) Wrestling

7. In a game of darts, how many points does a player score if he/she lands a dart on the bull's-eye?
   a) 20 points
   b) 50 points
   c) 100 points

8. According to major boxing organizations, the upper limit of which class of weight is 105 pounds?
   a) Flyweight
   b) Minimumweight
   c) Cruiserweight

9. Basketball gets its name from the ___ baskets which James Naismith, the inventor of the sport, used for that first game played in 1891. Fill in the blank.
   a) Grape
   b) Apple
   c) Peach

10. Whiff Whaff and Flim Flam are some of the names of which sport?
    a) Table Tennis
    b) Squash
    c) Volleyball

FUN TO KNOW

Squash has been around since 1830. It was invented by students at the Harrow School outside London.

Volleyball was invented in 1895 by William G. Morgan. It was designed as an indoor sport for businessmen who found the new game of basketball too vigorous.

INSECTS

1. Which of these is a quick-moving, slender, flat, wingless insect having three tail bristles and scales?
   a) Cockroach
   b) Silverfish
   c) Lice

2. Which is the largest order of insects, representing about 40 per cent of the known insect species?
   a) Coleoptera
   b) Zoraptera
   c) Lepidoptera

3. An immature form of an insect that does not change greatly as it grows, is called a...
   a) Cocoon
   b) Nymph
   c) Annelid

4. Houseflies find sugar with which parts of their bodies?
   a) Wings
   b) Antennae
   c) Feet

5. Zika virus, West Nile virus, Chikungunya virus spread to people by the bite of an infected...
   a) Mosquito
   b) Wasp
   c) Flea

6. Which insect does not have a mouth or a digestive system because it only lives for about a week after leaving the cocoon and does not eat?
   a) Luna Moth
   b) Praying Mantis
   c) Madagascar Hissing Cockroach

7. Which of these is one of the chemical substances that helps to produce light, with almost no heat, in fireflies?
   a) Galactose
   b) Benzene
   c) Luciferin

8. The giant weta, considered to be the heaviest insect in the world, is found only in...
   a) New Zealand
   b) France
   c) India

9. Male members of which insect family produce loud noises by vibrating membranes (timbals) near the base of the abdomen?
   a) Cicada
   b) Dung Beetle
   c) Bed Bug

10. Which author collected butterflies and discovered and named a new subspecies, the Karner Blue butterfly?
    a) William Faulkner
    b) Vladimir Nabokov
    c) Stephen King

FUN TO KNOW

The wingless midge, *Belgica antarctica*, is the only insect and fully terrestrial animal endemic to Antarctica.

Cockroaches are among the most primitive living, winged insects, appearing today much like they do in fossils that are more than 320 million years old.

INVENTIONS AND DISCOVERIES

1. In 2012, which of these was named as the most important invention in the history of food by the Royal Society of UK?
   a) Refrigerator
   b) Microwave Oven
   c) Mixer Grinder

2. Maurice LeBlanc's article in the journal *La Lumière électrique* was the basis of all future...
   a) Gramophones
   b) Televisions
   c) Vacuum Cleaners

3. With whose invention would you associate US Patent Number 174,465?
   a) Alexander Graham Bell
   b) Thomas Alva Edison
   c) Samuel Morse

4. According to Albert Einstein, what is the 'mother of all invention'?
   a) Necessity
   b) Passion
   c) Hunger

5. Who proved that a rocket will work in a vacuum and needs no air to push against?

a) Howard Florey
b) Alexander Parkes
c) Robert H. Goddard

6. The Nobel Prize in Physiology or Medicine 1923 went for the discovery of which of these?
   a) Human blood groups
   b) Insulin
   c) Vitamin K

7. Whose invention, originally named the Eterpen, received its first bulk order from the Royal Air Force?
   a) Jethro Tull
   b) Laszlo Biro
   c) Ivan Pavlov

8. An image of which of these helped Wilhelm Conrad Röntgen in his discovery of X-ray?
   a) His pet dog's face
   b) His daughter's eyes
   c) His wife's hand

9. Who conceived the idea of the instant camera in 1943?
   a) Thomas Edison
   b) Edwin H. Land
   c) Peter Durand

10. The earliest mention of which of these machines is in a lawsuit filed in Strasbourg in 1439?
    a) Mobile phone
    b) Printing press
    c) Computer

> **FUN TO KNOW**
>
> The microwave oven was discovered after Percy Spencer noticed that a candy bar had melted in his pocket while he was working in a lab testing magnetrons, the high-powered vacuum tubes inside radars.
>
> Hiroshi Ueda invented the selfie stick when a child, who he had asked to click a picture of his wife and himself in the Louvre Museum in Paris, ran away with his camera.

ISLANDS

1. Erik the Red was the founder of the first European settlement on...
   a) Sumatra
   b) Greenland
   c) Madagascar

2. The national flag of which country features the silhouette of an island above two green olive branches?
   a) Indonesia
   b) Cyprus
   c) Maldives

3. In which 2000 film did Tom Hanks play a man stranded on an uninhabited Pacific island?
   a) *Back to the Future*
   b) *The Way*
   c) *Cast Away*

4. The Galapagos Islands are named after which creature?
   a) Elephant
   b) Crocodile
   c) Tortoise

5. Which island country was referred to as Taprobane by ancient Greek geographers?

a) Japan
   b) Sri Lanka
   c) Maldives

6. On which island would you find the giant moai statues?
   a) Christmas Island
   b) Cook Islands
   c) Easter Island

7. Whose third voyage takes him to the flying island of Laputa?
   a) Sindbad
   b) Gulliver
   c) Robinson Crusoe

8. Which country, located southwest of Sri Lanka, is made up of 1,102 islands?
   a) Maldives
   b) Indonesia
   c) Japan

9. Proboscis monkeys are endemic to the jungles of...
   a) Madagascar
   b) Borneo
   c) New Guinea

10. Which painter is famous for his self-imposed exile in Tahiti, French Polynesia?
    a) Edvard Munch
    b) Henri Matisse
    c) Paul Gauguin

FUN TO KNOW

The two principal parts of the Niagara falls—the Horseshoe Falls adjoining the Canadian bank and the American Falls adjoining the American bank—are separated by Goat Island.

The only active volcano in India is located on Barren Island, Andaman and Nicobar Islands.

KINGS AND QUEENS

1. Whose record did Queen Elizabeth II break to become the longest reigning British monarch?
   a) Queen Victoria
   b) Mary II
   c) George VI

2. King Bhumibol Adulyadej or Rama IX was the monarch of...
   a) Bhutan
   b) Japan
   c) Thailand

3. Which Mughal emperor built Fatehpur Sikri in honour of Shaikh Salim Chishti?
   a) Akbar
   b) Shah Jahan
   c) Babur

4. Qūb al-Dén Mubārak Shah was the last emperor of which dynasty?
   a) Mughal
   b) Khalji
   c) Lodhi

5. In 1922, whose tomb, KV 62, was discovered in the Valley of the Kings?
   a) Charlemagne

b) Alexander the Great
c) Tutankhamen

6. Who was formally known as Gaius Julius Caesar Octavianus?
   a) Hannibal
   b) Augustus
   c) Nero

7. Who was the fifteenth and last child of Holy Roman Emperor Francis I and the powerful Habsburg Empress Maria Theresa?
   a) Maria Theresa
   b) Maria Amalia
   c) Marie Antoinette

8. Whose successors on the throne of Delhi were Muizuddin Bahram and Ala-ud-din Masud?
   a) Razia Sultan
   b) Chand Bibi
   c) Nur Jehan

9. Which queen was born as Manikarnika?
   a) Rani Padmini
   b) Rani Lakshmibai
   c) Jodha Bai

10. Whose greatest victory was at the Battle of Gaugamela, now northern Iraq, in 331 BC?
    a) King George II
    b) Akbar
    c) Alexander the Great

FUN TO KNOW

The King of Bhutan is known as Druk Gyalpo or the Dragon King. Ugyen Wangchuck was the first Druk Gyalpo. He established the Wangchuck dynasty that rules till date.

At the end of World War II, Hirohito publicly renounced his divinity as part of the terms of surrender of Japan.

LANGUAGES

1. In which month is International Mother Language Day observed by the United Nations?
   a) January
   b) February
   c) March

2. Which is the common official language of Niger, Senegal and Benin?
   a) French
   b) English
   c) Spanish

3. In 2010, which of these became the second official language of Uttarakhand?
   a) Tamil
   b) Sanskrit
   c) Pali

4. Klingon is the language of a member of a war-like humanoid alien species in...
   a) *The Flintstones*
   b) *Star Trek*
   c) *Dr Who*

5. Which language was used for Buddhist works because the Buddha opposed the use of Sanskrit?
   a) Pali

b) Telugu
   c) Tamil

6. Dzongkha is the official language of...
   a) Vietnam
   b) Thailand
   c) Bhutan

7. In the English language most words begin with the letter...
   a) M
   b) P
   c) S

8. Who created the fictional language Newspeak, which has words like 'joycamp' and 'ungood'?
   a) George Orwell
   b) J.R.R. Tolkien
   c) George R.R. Martin

9. Which is the last language to be found on the language panel of a Indian currency note?
   a) Urdu
   b) Telugu
   c) Odia

10. A language that is adopted as a common language between speakers whose native languages are different, is called the...
    a) Vox populi
    b) Lingua franca
    c) Laissez-faire

FUN TO KNOW

The Greeks called the Egyptian script that they found on temple walls and public monuments, Hieroglyphics. Most of the pictures can stand for the object they represent, but usually they stand for sounds.

IsiZulu, IsiXhosa, Afrikaans, English, Sepedi, Setswana, Sesotho, Xitsonga, siSwati, Tshivenda and IsiNdebele are the official languages of South Africa.

LAST WORDS

1. 'I have offended God and mankind because my work didn't reach the quality it should have' are the famous last words of which Italian artist?
   a) Michelangelo
   b) Leonardo da Vinci
   c) Raphael

2. Who famously prophesied his own death the night before and said, 'Tomorrow, at sunrise, I shall no longer be here'?
   a) Nostradamus
   b) Socrates
   c) Aristotle

3. Complete the last words of Caesar in Shakespeare's *Julius Caesar*, 'Et tu, _____?'
   a) Casca
   b) Cassius
   c) Brute

4. Writer T.S. Eliot was only able to whisper one word as he died: 'Valerie', the name of his....
   a) Daughter
   b) Wife
   c) Mother

5. Which famous personality's last words were, 'Oh

wow. Oh wow. Oh wow'?
a) Steve Jobs
b) Nikola Tesla
c) Alexander Graham Bell

6. What were Goethe's last words?
a) 'Books! More books!'
b) 'Light! More light!'
c) 'Time! More time!'

7. Name the former President of India who said, 'Funny guy! Are you doing well?'
a) V.V. Giri
b) S. Radhakrishnan
c) A.P.J. Abdul Kalam

8. Whose last words were, 'I shall hear in heaven'?
a) Bach
b) Beethoven
c) Chopin

9. Before Sir Winston Churchill slipped into a coma from which he never awoke he said…
a) 'I'm bored with it all.'
b) 'I'm bored now.'
c) 'I'm tired of it.'

10. Who said, 'Go on, get out! Last words are for fools who haven't said enough!'?
a) Vladimir Lenin
b) Karl Marx
c) Adolf Hitler

FUN TO KNOW

After Marie Antoinette accidentally stepped on her executioner's foot as she climbed the scaffold to the guillotine, she reportedly said, 'Pardonnez-moi, monsieur. Je ne l'ai pas fait exprès', which translates to 'Pardon me, sir. I did not do it on purpose.'

When Benjamin Franklin's daughter asked him to change position in bed so he could breathe more easily, Franklin's reply was, 'A dying man can do nothing easy.'

LIGHT

1. The name of which chemical element that glows in the dark, comes from the Greek words meaning 'light bringing'?
   a) Cadmium
   b) Phosphorus
   c) Antimony

2. 'They danced by the light of the moon': This is the last line of which poem?
   a) 'The Owl and the Pussy-Cat'
   b) 'Wynken, Blynken and Nod'
   c) 'The Crocodile'

3. A natural phenomenon of coloured lights that appears in the high latitudes of the Northern Hemisphere, is known as...
   a) Aurora Australis
   b) Aurora Meteoric
   c) Aurora Borealis

4. Which of these names mean 'mountain of light'?
   a) Kohinoor
   b) Mumtaz Mahal
   c) Hayat Baksh

5. In its simplest form, quantum theory describes light as consisting of discrete packets of energy called...

a) Protons
b) Photons
c) Poltoons

6. Who was called the 'Lady with the Lamp' by the British soldiers who were wounded in the Crimean War?
   a) Elizabeth Blackwell
   b) Joan of Arc
   c) Florence Nightingale

7. The first commercially viable incandescent light bulb, patented by Thomas Edison in 1880, used a filament made from...
   a) Burnt bamboo
   b) Pine needle
   c) Fish bone

8. Which of these cells in the eye are active at higher light levels and are capable of colour vision?
   a) Cones
   b) Spheres
   c) Rods

9. Who said, 'How far that little candle throws his beams! So shines a good deed in a weary world'?
   a) Jane Austen
   b) John Milton
   c) William Shakespeare

10. On whose death did Jawaharlal Nehru remark, 'The light has gone out of our lives...'?
    a) Mahatma Gandhi
    b) Subhas Chandra Bose
    c) Rajendra Prasad

> **FUN TO KNOW**
>
> At least a quarter of us respond to bright lights by sneezing. This is called the photic sneeze reflex or ACHOO syndrome (Autosomal dominant Compelling Helio-Ophthalmic Outburst).
>
> The giant squid, *Taningia danae*, has the largest light-producing organs of any living creature.

MAGICAL NUMBERS

1. The elements of the sequence of numbers 1, 1, 2, 3, 5, 8, 13, 21, ..., each of which, after the second, is the sum of the two previous numbers are called...
   a) Planck's Constant
   b) Fibonacci numbers
   c) The Golden Ratio

2. Who gave the title *8½* to a film after he had directed six solo films and three collaborations (counting as a half each)?
   a) Federico Fellini
   b) Sergei M. Eisenstein
   c) Ingmar Bergman

3. According to *The Hitchhiker's Guide to the Galaxy*, what is the answer to the 'Ultimate Question of Life, the Universe, and Everything'?
   a) 35
   b) 42
   c) 57

4. Which of these names is a play on the mathematical expression for the number 1 followed by 100 zeros?
   a) Yahoo
   b) Google
   c) Bing

5. The spots on the opposite sides of a dice always add up to...
   a) Six
   b) Seven
   c) Eight

6. Which of these phrases refers to a state of total confusion?
   a) Pieces of eight
   b) At sixes and sevens
   c) On cloud nine

7. The title of the novel *Fahrenheit 451* refers to the temperature at which...
   a) Chocolate melts
   b) Paper catches fire and burns
   c) Water boils

8. Which is the only number whose square can be produced simply by adding 1 and whose reciprocal by subtracting 1?
   a) The Golden Ratio
   b) Pi
   c) The Coupling Constant

9. What is a positive integer that is equal to the sum of its proper divisors called?
   a) Real number
   b) Perfect number
   c) Magical number

10. Adele named her albums 19, 21 and 25 after her...
    a) Favourite numbers
    b) Age at the time of the release of the albums
    c) The number of songs in each album

> **FUN TO KNOW**
>
> A myth surrounding the origin of the fear of the number 13 involves one of the oldest legal documents in the world—the Code of Hammurabi. It is said that the 13th law from its list of legal rules had been omitted.
>
> The Beijing Olympics began at 8.08 p.m. local time, on the eighth day of the eighth month of the year 2008.

MONEY

1. In which country was paper money first used?
   a) UK
   b) China
   c) India

2. 'I declare after all there is no enjoyment like reading!' This quote from a famous book appears on a banknote of which country?
   a) USA
   b) UK
   c) New Zealand

3. Who has a Dollarmatian dog?
   a) Richie Rich
   b) Popeye
   c) Tintin

4. Ngultrum is the currency of which country?
   a) Bhutan
   b) Nepal
   c) Sri Lanka

5. Who wrote, *Not a Penny More, Not a Penny Less*?
   a) Agatha Christie
   b) Jeffrey Archer
   c) Sidney Sheldon

6. In which city was the first ATM installed?
   a) London
   b) Paris
   c) Berlin

7. *The Color of Money* is a 1986 film directed by...
   a) Martin Scorsese
   b) Steven Spielberg
   c) Woody Allen

8. The name of which Shakespearean character is used to describe a moneylender who charges extremely high rates of interest?
   a) Shylock
   b) Macbeth
   c) Othello

9. In 1696, who was appointed Warden of the Royal Mint in the UK on the recommendation of Charles Montague?
   a) Robert Boyle
   b) Charles Darwin
   c) Isaac Newton

10. Fill in the blank to complete this proverb: A ____ and his money are soon parted.
    a) Coward
    b) Miser
    c) Fool

FUN TO KNOW

The word money comes from the Latin moneta, title of the goddess Juno, in whose temple in Rome money was minted.

Bitcoin is a digital currency that uses rules of cryptography for regulation and generation of units of currency. It was invented by Satoshi Nakamoto in 2009.

MUSIC

1. Which song by Stevie Wonder won the 1985 Oscar in the Best Original Song category?
   a) 'You are the Sunshine of My Life'
   b) 'Master Blaster'
   c) 'I Just Called To Say I Love You'

2. Who was the first musician ever to be awarded the Bharat Ratna?
   a) M.S. Subbulakshmi
   b) Kishore Kumar
   c) R.D. Burman

3. Right before settling for The Beatles, what was the name of the band?
   a) Silver Beatles
   b) Black Beatles
   c) Red Beatles

4. Which band broke up after their drummer, John Bonham, passed away in 1980?
   a) Pink Floyd
   b) Led Zeppelin
   c) The Eagles

5. How do we better know Stefani Joanne Angelina Germanotta?
   a) Adele

b) Lady Gaga
c) Sia

6. As of 2017, who holds the record of winning the highest number of Filmfare Awards in the Best Male Playback Singer category ?
   a) R.D. Burman
   b) Kishore Kumar
   c) Manna Dey

7. Which band was formed by guitarist Malcolm Young after his previous band, the Velvet Underground, failed?
   a) Iron Maiden
   b) Metallica
   c) AC/DC

8. Neverland Ranch was the popular address of which singer?
   a) John Lennon
   b) Michael Jackson
   c) Elvis Presley

9. In 2011, who entered the Guinness World Records for the most single studio recordings?
   a) Lata Mangeshkar
   b) Sunidhi Chauhan
   c) Asha Bhosle

10. After which musician is the airport in Liverpool named?
    a) David Gilmour
    b) John Lennon
    c) Mark Knopfler

> **FUN TO KNOW**
>
> In 2009, A.R. Rahman won the Oscar and the Golden Globe Award for his work in *Slumdog Millionaire*. In 2011, he was yet again nominated for the Oscars in two categories for his work in the film *127 Hours*.
>
> Simon & Garfunkel initially named themselves Tom and Jerry—Tom Graph and Jerry Landis.

NATIONAL FLAGS

1. Which is the only country in the modern world that does not have a rectangular or square national flag?
   a) Qatar
   b) Nepal
   c) Chile

2. On the national flag of which country would you find a globe with 27 white five-pointed stars?
   a) Chile
   b) Ghana
   c) Brazil

3. What does the colour red on the national flag of Iceland stand for?
   a) Volcanic fires
   b) Roses
   c) Ice

4. The scroll on the national flag of Spain bears the motto 'Plus Ultra', which means...
   a) Truly Beyond
   b) Further Beyond
   c) Freedom Beyond

5. Which symbol is common to the national flags of Japan and Bangladesh?

a) Square
b) Triangle
c) Circle

6. What is the sun bearing a human face on the national flag of Uruguay called?
   a) Sun of May
   b) Sun of June
   c) Sun of April

7. The national flag of which country is known as 'Le drapeau tricolore'?
   a) Italy
   b) France
   c) Spain

8. On the national flag of which country would you find a blue star called Magen David?
   a) Italy
   b) Ghana
   c) Israel

9. According to Dr S. Radhakrishnan, which colour on the national flag of India denotes renunciation or disinterestedness?
   a) Green
   b) Saffron
   c) White

10. The Eagle of Saladin appears on the national flag of which country?
    a) Eritrea
    b) Ethiopia
    c) Egypt

FUN TO KNOW

The national flag of India was adopted on 22 July 1947 and was designed by Pingali Venkayya.

The national flag of United Kingdom is commonly called the Union Jack.

NOBEL PRIZE

1. In 1953, in which category did Winston Churchill receive the Nobel Prize?
    a) Peace
    b) Literature
    c) Economics

2. Who initially accepted the Nobel Prize but was later coerced by the authorities of the Soviet Union, his native country, to decline it?
    a) Svetlana Alexievich
    b) Boris Pasternak
    c) Andre Geim

3. The central bank of which country established the Prize in Economic Sciences in memory of Alfred Nobel?
    a) Denmark
    b) Norway
    c) Sweden

4. Malala Yousafzai set which record in 2014?
    a) Only person from Pakistan to win a Nobel Prize
    b) First Asian woman to win a Nobel Prize
    c) Youngest Nobel Prize winner

5. Who was the first person to receive the Nobel Prize in Physics?

a) C.V. Raman
   b) Wilhelm Conrad Röntgen
   c) Guglielmo Marconi

6. Who was the only person to have been awarded two unshared Nobel Prizes—the 1954 Nobel Prize in Chemistry and the 1962 Nobel Peace Prize?
   a) Linus Pauling
   b) Ernest Rutherford
   c) Klas Pontus Arnoldson

7. Who among these has been awarded the Nobel Prize?
   a) Dmitri Mendeleev
   b) Edwin Hubble
   c) Guglielmo Marconi

8. In which category has the Nobel Prize been shared by two laureates the least number of times?
   a) Peace
   b) Literature
   c) Chemistry

9. In 2012, who delivered the acceptance speech for the Nobel Peace Prize more than two decades after it was awarded?
   a) Aung San Suu Kyi
   b) Pablo Neruda
   c) Malala Yousafzai

10. In 1902, who received the Nobel Prize in Physiology or Medicine for his work on malaria?
    a) Edward Jenner
    b) Ronald Ross
    c) Louis Pasteur

> **FUN TO KNOW**
>
> A member of the Swedish parliament nominated Adolf Hitler for the Nobel Peace Prize in 1939.
>
> Rabindranath Tagore was the first Asian to win the Nobel Prize. The Nobel Prize medal, received by him in 1913, was stolen in 2004 from a museum of Visva Bharati University.

OSCARS

1. Kathryn Bigelow is the first woman to win an Oscar in which category?
   a) Best Director
   b) Best Costume Design
   c) Best Film Editing

2. The Oscar statuette comprises a knight standing on a...
   a) Camera
   b) Bell
   c) Reel of film

3. Which Indian film lost to *Nights in Cabiria* by one vote in the Best Foreign Language Film category?
   a) *Lagaan*
   b) *Mother India*
   c) *Mughal-e-Azam*

4. Who won the first Academy Award for Best Actor?
   a) Peter O'Toole
   b) Emil Jannings
   c) Charlie Chaplin

5. Who became the first actress to win an Academy Award for playing another Academy Award winner?
   a) Kate Winslet

b) Cate Blanchett
c) Julia Roberts

6. In 1953, who became the most honoured male at a single ceremony?
   a) John Ford
   b) Alfred Hitchcock
   c) Walt Disney

7. In 1971, George C. Scott became the first actor to reject the Academy Award for Best Actor for which film?
   a) *Gone with the Wind*
   b) *The Changeling*
   c) *Patton*

8. Heath Ledger and Peter Finch have...
   a) Starred in three films nominated for Best Picture the same year
   b) Have been given the award posthumously
   c) Been nominated eight times but never won an Oscar

9. Who among these directors has never won an Academy Award in the Best Director category?
   a) Steven Spielberg
   b) Clint Eastwood
   c) Alfred Hitchcock

10. In 2013, Quvenzhane Wallis became the youngest to be nominated for Best Actress in a Leading Role for her role in which film?
    a) *Beasts of the Southern Wild*
    b) *The Artist*
    c) *Bridesmaids*

FUN TO KNOW

Due to metal shortage during World War II, the Oscar statuettes were made of painted plaster for three years.

In 2013, for the first time Academy members were able to vote online.

PAINTERS

1. According to art critics, the adult career of which Spanish painter can be divided into the 'Blue Period', the 'Rose Period' and the 'Classic Period'?
   a) Edvard Munch
   b) Pablo Picasso
   c) Raphael

2. Who painted the vast fresco of *The Last Judgement* on the end altar wall of the Sistine Chapel between 1536 and 1541?
   a) Salvador Dali
   b) Michelangelo
   c) Rembrandt

3. Which of these artists restricted his/her palette to seven colours: Indian red, yellow ochre, cadmium green, vermillion, grey, blue and white?
   a) Amrita Sher-Gill
   b) Nicholas Roerich
   c) Jamini Roy

4. In 1984, which painter designed the Belgium embassy in New Delhi?
   a) Satish Gujral
   b) Manjit Bawa
   c) M.F. Husain

5. Who began working on *Noa Noa*, a book project based on his Tahitian experience, after he returned to Europe in 1893?
   a) Paul Gaugin
   b) Henri Matisse
   c) Claude Monet

6. Which of these is a painting by Salvador Dali featuring ants and melting watches?
   a) *The Persistence of Memory*
   b) *Guernica*
   c) *The Sampling Officials*

7. In 1894, who set up a lithographic press in order to mass-produce copies of his paintings as oleographs?
   a) Raja Ravi Verma
   b) Abanindranath Tagore
   c) S.H. Raza

8. The *Codex Leicester*, bought by Bill Gates, contains which painter's studies on hydraulics and the movement of water?
   a) Michelangelo
   b) Vincent van Gogh
   c) Leonardo da Vinci

9. The paintings in Shashi Tharoor's *Kerala: God's Own Country* are by which famous painter?
   a) Amrita Sher-Gil
   b) Jamini Roy
   c) M.F. Husain

10. Whose 1872 painting, *Impression, Sunrise*, inspired French critic Louis Leroy to give the Impressionist movement its name?
    a) Pierre-Auguste Renoir
    b) Claude Monet
    c) Paul Gauguin

> **FUN TO KNOW**
>
> Rabindranath Tagore's artistic adventure began with doodles that turned crossed-out words and lines into images.
>
> Each page of the Constitution of India was beautifully decorated by the artist Nandalal Bose and his students.

PRECIOUS STONES

1. The word 'garnet' is said to have come from the French word for...
   a) Strawberry
   b) Pomegranate
   c) Grapefruit

2. Sir Walter Scott's 1829 novel, *Anne of Geierstein*, gave which gemstone the reputation of being unlucky?
   a) Emerald
   b) Topaz
   c) Opal

3. In Sanskrit, which gem is known as *Ratnaraj*, meaning the king of gems?
   a) Sapphire
   b) Diamond
   c) Ruby

4. 'The Adventure of the Blue Carbuncle' is a short story by...
   a) Arthur Conan Doyle
   b) Agatha Christie
   c) Edgar Allan Poe

5. Which continent is known to be the only source of tanzanite?

a) Asia
b) South America
c) Africa

6. *Padparadscha*, the Sinhalese word for lotus flower, is the name of a rare and valuable pinkish-orange...
    a) Ruby
    b) Sapphire
    c) Emerald

7. Ise-Shima National Park, famous for its cultured-pearl industry, is located in...
    a) China
    b) Japan
    c) India

8. Which chemical element is responsible for giving turquoise its colour?
    a) Copper
    b) Silver
    c) Gold

9. Which island is referred to as the Emerald Isle?
    a) Greenland
    b) Ireland
    c) Finland

10. Aquamarine gets its name from the Latin words for...
    a) Seawater
    b) Sea Fish
    c) Sea Monster

FUN TO KNOW

Rubies are formed of a mineral called corundum, made up of aluminium oxide. Its colour is a result of traces of chromium.

Diamonds can be burnt. If you heat a diamond between 1290–1650 degrees Fahrenheit it will burn.

SCIENCE FICTION

1. Who is the author of the story of the Martian attack on England where the unearthly creatures arrive in huge cylinders?
   a) Isaac Asimov
   b) H.G. Wells
   c) Arthur C. Clarke

2. In which book would you meet the characters Hal, the robot, and the astronaut David Bowman?
   a) *Hyperion*
   b) *2001: A Space Odyssey*
   c) *Brave New World*

3. In which book does Ylla dream of Captain Nathaniel York coming down in his rocket?
   a) *The Night*
   b) *The Martian Chronicles*
   c) *The Fog Horn*

4. Who propounded the 'Three Laws of Robotics' in *I, Robot*?
   a) Isaac Asimov
   b) H.G. Wells
   c) Robin Cook

5. In which novel by Mary Shelly was a monster created by the science student Victor?

a) *Frankenstein*
   b) *The Complete Robot*
   c) *The Strange Case of Dr Jekyll* and *Mr Hyde*

6. *Robbie, The Evitable Conflict* and *Reason* are parts of which of these works?
   a) *The Zap Gun*
   b) *I, Robot*
   c) *Do Androids Dream of Electric Sheep?*

7. In which book is melange, referred to as the 'spice of spices', essential for interstellar travel?
   a) *Dune*
   b) *1984*
   c) *Neuromancer*

8. Which fish from a Douglas Adam novel, when inserted into the ear, allowed one to understand any language?
   a) Giggle
   b) Toggle
   c) Babel

9. In the novel *The Time Machine*, the traveller finds himself in a world of Morlocks and...
   a) Eloi
   b) Inga
   c) Pilo

10. *'It was a bright cold day in April, and the clocks were striking thirteen'*—is the first opening line of which book?
   a) *Neuromancer*
   b) *Dune*
   c) *Nineteen Eighty-Four*

> **FUN TO KNOW**
>
> The annual Nebula Awards recognizes the best works in science fiction.
>
> In 1926, writer Hugo Gernsback founded *Amazing Stories*, said to be the first true science-fiction magazine.

SEQUELS AND PREQUELS

1. As of 2017, other than *The Lord of the Rings: The Return of the King*, which is the only sequel to have won the Academy Award in the Best Picture category?
   a) *The Godfather Part II*
   b) *Indiana Jones and the Last Crusade*
   c) *Mission Impossible 2*

2. In the sequel of which of these films would you meet Puss in Boots?
   a) *Ratatouille*
   b) *Shrek*
   c) *The Lion King*

3. Which was the first Hindi film to be shown at the United Nations?
   a) *Dhoom 3*
   b) *Kahaani 2*
   c) *Lage Raho Munnabhai*

4. Brian De Palma, John Woo, J.J. Abrams, Brad Bird and Christopher McQuarrie — each of them directed a film from this film franchise. Name the first film of the franchise.
   a) *Harry Potter and the Sorcerer's Stone*
   b) *Saw*
   c) *Mission Impossible*

5. The prequel to the television show *Breaking Bad* is named after which character from the show?
   a) Skyler White
   b) Walter White
   c) Saul Goodman

6. A key sequence in the third film of the Batman series, *The Dark Knight Rises*, was shot in which of these popular spots in India?
   a) Mehrangarh Fort
   b) Taj Mahal
   c) Gateway of India

7. The sequel to which of these films was based on Walter Wager's novel *58 Minutes*?
   a) *Die Hard*
   b) *Terminator*
   c) *Sixth Sense*

8. With which film franchise would you associate the titles *A New Hope, The Empire Strikes Back* and *Attack of the Clones*?
   a) Star Trek
   b) The Lord of the Rings
   c) Star Wars

9. In the Bourne film series, out of the five films only one does not have Matt Damon playing the lead character. Which is that film?
   a) *The Bourne Ultimatum*
   b) *The Bourne Supremacy*
   c) *The Bourne Legacy*

10. Which film became the first Indian film to have earned Rs 1,000 crore internationally?
    a) *Bahubali 2: The Conclusion*
    b) *Dhoom 2*
    c) *Krrish 3*

FUN TO KNOW

The sequel to the novel *To Kill a Mockingbird* was released 55 years later, in 2015. It is titled *Go Set a Watchman*.

The Harry Potter film series has eight instalments but none has ever won an Academy Award.

SOCIAL MEDIA

1. In 2011, what did Zuckerberg introduce as 'all your stories, all your apps and a new way to express who you are'?
   a) Scrapbook
   b) Wall
   c) Timeline

2. Which of these, co-founded by Evan Spiegel and Bobby Murphy, was initially called Picaboo?
   a) Snapchat
   b) Instagram
   c) Flickr

3. Jan Koum keeps a handwritten note which reads, 'No Ads! No Games! No Gimmicks!' on his desk, which was also the idea behind his startup venture. He is the co-founder of...
   a) Facebook
   b) WhatsApp
   c) Google+

4. What is the blue bird of the Twitter logo called?
   a) Larry
   b) Barry
   c) Harry

5. In 2014, which music video surpassed the YouTube viewing limit?
   a) *Gangnam Style*
   b) *Wrecking Ball*
   c) *Dark Horse*

6. Adam D'Angelo quit his job as the Chief Technical Officer of Facebook to start which of these?
   a) Quora
   b) Pinterest
   c) Instagram

7. The name 'Instagram' is a combination of the words 'instant' and which other word?
   a) Hologram
   b) Telegram
   c) Program

8. In the early 2000s, Tom Anderson became the first default friend of whoever joined…
   a) Orkut
   b) Myspace
   c) Facebook

3. Which of these started out in the living room of co-founder Reid Hoffman in 2002?
   a) YouTube
   b) LinkedIn
   c) Myspace

10. 'What is red, is a planet and is the focus of my orbit?'—was a tweet from....
    a) Curiosity Rover
    b) Chandrayaan II
    c) Mars Orbiter

> **FUN TO KNOW**
>
> The first ever video posted on YouTube was of YouTube co-founder Jawed Karim and it lasted for 18 seconds. The caption of the video was *Me at the Zoo*.
>
> Facebook's main colour is blue because Mark Zuckerberg has colour blindness. In an interview, he told the reporter 'blue is the richest colour for me—I can see all of blue.'

SPORTS IN FILMS

1. In the film *Chak de! India*, the Indian women's hockey team play in the finals of which tournament?
   a) The Olympics
   b) The World Cup
   c) The Commonwealth Games

2. In which 2015 film was Michael B. Jordan's character trained by Sylvester Stallone's Rocky Balboa?
   a) *Never Back Down*
   b) *Warrior*
   c) *Creed*

3. The film *Tin Cup* revolves around which sport?
   a) Polo
   b) Golf
   c) Swimming

4. Which film on football stars Parminder Nagra and Keira Knightley in the lead roles?
   a) *Bend It Like Beckham*
   b) *Goal*
   c) *Escape to Victory*

5. Who directed the biography that focuses on the triumphs and controversies of sporting legend Muhammad Ali, and stars Will Smith in the title role?

a) Steven Spielberg
b) Michael Mann
c) Christopher Nolan

6. The 2016 film *Dangal* was based on the life of Mahavir Singh Phogat who is a former...
   a) Wrestler
   b) Boxer
   c) Footballer

7. In which film do the people of a small village in Victorian India stake their future on a game of cricket against their ruthless British rulers?
   a) *Lagaan: Once Upon a Time in India*
   b) *Sultan*
   c) *Patiala House*

8. Which film revoles around three men, Red Pollard, Charles S. Howard, and Tom Smith who are the principle jockey, owner, and trainer of a championship horse?
   a) *Jerry Maguire*
   b) *War Horse*
   c) *Seabiscuit*

9. Who plays the title role in the film *Coach Carter*?
   a) Morgan Freeman
   b) Laurence Fishburne
   c) Samuel L. Jackson

10. Complete the name of the following sports film: *Remember the* _____.
    a) *Titans*
    b) *Giants*
    c) *Trolls*

> **FUN TO KNOW**
>
> In *Space Jam*, the Looney Tunes seek the aid of retired basketball champion, Michael Jordan so that they could win a basketball match and earn their freedom.
>
> Milkha Singh is said to have taken just one rupee from Rakeysh Omprakash Mehra to allow him to make a film on his life.

SWEETMEATS

1. Which of these are sometimes known as 'tipsy cakes'?
   a) Trifles
   b) Cheesecakes
   c) Bebinca

2. Which of these is traditionally eaten on Good Friday?
   a) Lemon tarts
   b) Hot cross buns
   c) Apple pies

3. Which of these is a small fried cake of sweetened dough, typically in the shape of a ball or ring?
   a) Sundae
   b) Fudge
   c) Doughnut

4. Which of these desserts, consisting of meringue with fruit and cream, was named after a Russian ballerina?
   a) Charlotte
   b) Pavlova
   c) Madeleine

5. Nobin Chandra prepared which sweet for Maharani Swarnamoyee Devi, the dowager of the house of

Cossimbazar, to excite her jaded palate?
a) Aabaar Khabo
b) Rasgulla
c) Kalakand

6. Tiramisu gets its name from an Italian word that means...
   a) Pick me up
   b) Sweet tooth
   c) After the meal

7. Which of these desserts is believed to have been invented out of a way to use up unused bread in nineteenth-century Mughal cuisines?
   a) Shahi Tukda
   b) Balushahi
   c) Shrikhand

8. Moon cake is a traditional food item of which country?
   a) Pakistan
   b) Egypt
   c) China

9. Oxford Dictionary defines which of these as 'a dessert originating in the Middle East made of filo pastry filled with chopped nuts and soaked in honey'?
   a) Falafel
   b) Baklava
   c) Baba Ghanoush

10. Which of these are also called Makkhan Vada in many parts of the country?
    a) Balushahi
    b) Ghevar
    c) Kalakand

> **FUN TO KNOW**
>
> It is believed that Bebinca was invented by a nun named Bibiona. Her first version had seven layers to represent the seven hills of Lisbon and Old Goa.
>
> The word 'dessert' comes from a French word that means 'clear the table'.

TELEVISION

1. Which show was originally called Insomnia Cafe and Six of One before getting its actual title?
   a) *Friends*
   b) *Desperate Housewives*
   c) *Seinfeld*

2. What is unusual about *Bleep My Dad Says*?
   a) It is based on a Twitter feed
   b) It has only one character
   c) It is a silent serial

3. Which series is set in the street of Wisteria Lane in the fictional American town of Fairview in Eagle State?
   a) *Desperate Housewives*
   b) *Modern Family*
   c) *How I Met Your Mother*

4. Which series is named after a character in George Orwell's 1949 novel, *Nineteen Eighty-Four*?
   a) *Big Brother*
   b) *Modern Family*
   c) *House of Cards*

5. According to the Guinness Book of World Records, which was the first game show on TV?
   a) *Who Wants to Be a Millionaire*

b) *Spelling Bee*
c) *Mastermind*

6. Which actress connects the TV series *Hum Paanch* and the Bengali film *Bhalo Theko*?
   a) Vidya Balan
   b) Anushka Sharma
   c) Priyanka Chopra

7. Which TV personality founded Harpo Productions in 1986?
   a) Oprah Winfrey
   b) Ed Sullivan
   c) Ellen DeGeneres

8. In which series would you meet ACP Pradyuman, Abhijeet, Daya, Inspector Fredricks, Dr Salunkhe and Dr Tarika?
   a) *CID*
   b) *India's Most Wanted*
   c) *Savdhaan India*

9. The Bazinga rieki jellyfish is named after the photographer who captured it on camera and the catchphrase made famous in...
   a) *The Big Bang Theory*
   b) *Stranger Things*
   c) *Breaking Bad*

10. With which TV show would you associate the catchprase, 'Yada, yada, yada'?
    a) *Family Matters*
    b) *Seinfeld*
    c) *The Simpsons*

> **FUN TO KNOW**
>
> In 1976, the then US president Gerald Ford was urged by fans of the Star Trek series to name the first NASA Space Shuttle 'Enterprise'. Their wish was granted but unfortunately, the Enterprise never reached space.
>
> A TV or radio drama serial revolving around the daily lives of a group of characters is called a soap opera because such serials were originally sponsored in the US by soap manufacturers.

TINTIN

1. What was the name of the children's weekly in which Tintin appeared for the first time in 1929?
   a) *Le Petit Vingtième*
   b) *Gazet van Antwerpen*
   c) *De Tijd*

2. Who among these is a villain in the Tintin comics?
   a) Bianca Castafiore
   b) Rastapopoulos
   c) Tarragon Hercules

3. In the French version of the Tintin adventures, *Destination Moon*, who is nicknamed 'The mammoth' by the spies?
   a) Professor Calculus
   b) Captain Haddock
   c) General Alcazar

4. Which international dignitary said, 'Deep down, my only international rival is Tintin'?
   a) President Charles de Gaulle
   b) President Barack Obama
   c) Prime Minister Manmohan Singh

5. What breed of dog is Tintin's faithful companion, Snowy?
   a) Pug

b) Beagle
c) Fox Terrier

6. In the 1936 book, *The Blue Lotus*, Tintin is assisted by a secret society called the...
   a) Sons of the Dragon
   b) Sons of the Tiger
   c) Sons of the Lotus

7. In which book did Tintin and Captain Haddock spend three hours in New Delhi in transit while waiting for an Air India flight to Kathmandu?
   a) *Tintin in Tibet*
   b) *The Secret of the Unicorn*
   c) *Land of Black Gold*

8. The 2011 film *The Adventures of Tintin: Secret of the Unicorn*, was directed by which legendary Hollywood director?
   a) Christopher Nolan
   b) George Lucas
   c) Steven Spielberg

9. With which character from the Tintin series would you associate the catchphrase 'blistering barnacles!'?
   a) Tintin
   b) Captain Haddock
   c) Professor Calculus

10. In the Hindi version of *The Adventures of Tintin* series, what were the names of detectives Thomson and Thompson?
    a) Santu and Bantu
    b) Motu and Patlu
    c) Ramesh and Suresh

> **FUN TO KNOW**
>
> In the 1954 book, *Explorers on the Moon*, Tintin and his dog Snowy travel to the moon on a rocket constructed by Professor Cuthbert Calculus. This was a good 15 years before US astronaut Neil Armstrong took that 'giant leap for mankind'.
>
> A total of 23 Tintin books were published during Hergé's lifetime. Another one was published after he passed away in 1983.

US PRESIDENTS

1. Who is the only president of the US to have a patent in his name for a device for 'buoying vessels over shoals'?
   a) James A. Garfield
   b) Abraham Lincoln
   c) Richard Nixon

2. The capital of which African country is named after the fifth US president, James Monroe?
   a) Tunisia
   b) Liberia
   c) Morocco

3. The autobiography of which president is titled *Dreams from My Father: A Story of Race and Inheritance*?
   a) John F. Kennedy
   b) Bill Clinton
   c) Barack Obama

4. Richard Nixon was the only president to have...
   a) Been re-elected for a third term
   b) Not resided in the White House
   c) Resigned from office

5. Which president of the United States has starred in films such as *Kings Row* and *Bedtime for Bonzo*?

a) Jimmy Carter
   b) Donald Trump
   c) Ronald Reagan

6. With which president would you associate the famous line 'Ask not what your country can do for you—ask what you can do for your country'?
   a) Thomas Jefferson
   b) John F. Kennedy
   c) Abraham Lincoln

7. In which TV show did candidates compete for a full-time job with Donald Trump?
   a) *The Profit*
   b) *Shark Tank*
   c) *The Apprentice*

8. Who was the first US president to win a Nobel Peace Prize?
   a) Theodore Roosevelt
   b) John F. Kennedy
   c) Jimmy Carter

9. Which president won the Grammy in the Best Spoken Word Album category for the audio book version of his memoir *A Full Life: Reflections at Ninety*?
   a) George W. Bush
   b) Jimmy Carter
   c) Ronald Reagan

10. Which president's son was the sixth president of the US?
    a) John Adams
    b) Harry S. Truman
    c) George W. Bush

FUN TO KNOW

President Franklin Roosevelt entertained guests with a premise for a mystery novel which was later adapted into a film, *The President's Mystery*. Franklin Roosevelt received a writing credit.

Alexander Graham Bell installed the first telephone in the White House during Rutherford B. Hayes's presidency. Its number was 'One'.

VIDEO GAMES

1. Name the prototype for the first multiplayer, multiprogram video game system designed by Ralph Baer.
   a) Brown Box
   b) Black Box
   c) Yellow Box

2. Which game, introduced by a Japanese arcade game manufacturer in 1980, had a central character that resembled a small pizza with a slice cut out?
   a) Dig Dug
   b) Pac-Man
   c) Pong

3. In the 1985 version of Super Mario Bros., what was the name of the evil king Mario and Luigi had to rescue Princess Toadstool from?
   a) Java
   b) Bowser
   c) Cursor

4. The name of which game comes from combining a Greek prefix that refers to the four squares contained in each block of the game and the word 'Tennis'?
   a) Tetris
   b) Terraria

c) Teslagrad

5. In 1997, the US Marine Corps converted monsters in which game into opposition forces and used the resulting game to train troops in tactics and communications?
   a) Half-Life
   b) Doom
   c) Quake

6. What is the name of the company that created the T-virus, in the Resident Evil series?
   a) The Raincoat Corporation
   b) The Umbrella Corporation
   c) The Trench Coat Corporation

7. Which game follows the adventures of theoretical physicist, Gordon Freeman, as numerous alien life forms invade the Black Mesa Federal Research Facility?
   a) Half-Life
   b) The Last of Us
   c) Space Invaders

8. Which shooting-based game, released in 1981 as a sequel to Galaxian, has players control a spacecraft at the bottom of the screen and attempt to shoot down squadrons of enemy ships?
   a) Galaga
   b) Space Invaders
   c) Alien

9. In which video game series would you come across the villainous Ganon and the Hyrule Kingdom?
   a) Super Mario Brothers
   b) The Legend of Zelda
   c) Sonic the Hedgehog

10. In 1974, the makers of the Magnavox Odyssey sued Atari for stealing the concept for which electronic game?
    a) Pong
    b) Donkey Kong
    c) Galaga

FUN TO KNOW

In 2015, the World Video Game Hall of Fame named 15 finalists for its inaugural class, a competitive list that included pioneering classics like Pong, Tetris and Super Mario Bros and contemporary hits like FIFA Soccer, Angry Birds and Minecraft.

The word atari comes from the ancient Japanese game of Go and means 'you are about to be engulfed'. Technically, it is the word used by a player to inform his opponent that he is about to lose, similar to 'check' in chess.

WIMBLEDON

1. Who was Sania Mirza's teammate when she became the first Indian woman to win the Wimbeldon doubles title?
   a) Martina Navratilova
   b) Martina Hingis
   c) Monica Seles

2. In 1985, Boris Becker became the first...
   a) Champion to retain his title
   b) Unseeded champion
   c) Non-European to win the men's singles title

3. At the 2010 Wimbeldon, Nicolas Mahut and John Isner played a first round singles match which was...
   a) The longest match in the history of the game
   b) The shortest match played in any tournament
   c) The only match played at the event

4. Which duo won the men's doubles Wimbledon Championships in 1999?
   a) Todd Woodbridge and Mark Woodforde
   b) Mahesh Bhupathi and Leander Paes
   c) Bob Bryan and Mike Bryan

5. With respect to Wimbledon, which of these happened for the first time in 1884?
   a) Cash prize was given

b) Women's Singles event started
c) The nine-point tiebreaker was introduced

6. In 2016, who became the first British men's singles winner at the Wimbledon since Fred Perry in 1936?
   a) Andy Murray
   b) Roger Federer
   c) Novak Djokovic

7. Who, besides Martina Navratilova, holds the record of winning 20 Wimbledon titles?
   a) Billie Jean King
   b) Boris Becker
   c) Pete Sampras

8. Who won the Wimbledon men's championship title each year from 1881 till 1886?
   a) Herbert Lawford
   b) Joshua Pim
   c) William Renshaw

9. Whose poem is inscribed above the entrance to Wimbledon's Centre Court?
   a) Rudyard Kipling
   b) William Wordsworth
   c) T.S. Eliot

10. Approximately 25–30 tons of which of these fruits is served during Wimbledon?
    a) Apple
    b) Strawberry
    c) Pomegranate

FUN TO KNOW

In 2007, for the first time, female winners received the same cash awards as the male winners.

Wimbledon is the only Grand Slam still played on grass courts.

WONDERFUL WORDS

1. Which term has its origin in a sketch by the British comedy group, Monty Python?
   a) Spam
   b) Byte
   c) Cache

2. Which word comes from the Greek words for terrible and lizard?
   a) Crocodile
   b) Capybara
   c) Dinosaur

3. Which term was coined in K. Čapek's play *R.U.R.*?
   a) Robot
   b) Computer
   c) Global Warming

4. Catamaran comes from a Tamil term which literally means 'tied wood'. It is a type of...
   a) Ladder
   b) Almirah
   c) Boat

5. *Karaoke* in Japanese literally means empty orchestra. It involves...
   a) Singing to pre-recorded music
   b) Dancing barefoot

c) Playing a musical instument

6. Who is said to have coined the words fashionable, cheap, dauntless and embrace?
   a) Charles Dickens
   b) William Shakespeare
   c) Mark Twain

7. Which word is derived from the name of a character in a 1960s Italian film titled *La Dolce Vita*?
   a) Villa
   b) Paparazzi
   c) Rendezvous

8. The name of which disease comes from two Italian words meaning 'bad air'?
   a) Dengue
   b) Malaria
   c) Anaemia

9. The word candidate comes from the Latin word *candidatus* meaning...
   a) High office
   b) White-robed
   c) Great commander

10. Which word has been used to refer to a person since 1613, to a machine since 1869, and to an electronic device since 1946?
    a) Computer
    b) Radio
    c) Telegraph

FUN TO KNOW

The word Juggernaut actually comes from Jagannatha, one of the names of the Hindu God, Vishnu.

Many comic book superheroes are actually 'alter egos' of normal characters. The term 'alter ego' means 'other self' in Latin.

ANSWERS

Animals in Fiction

1. *The Wind in the Willows*
2. Kiki
3. Mocha Dick
4. Napoleon
5. Mongoose
6. Mr Fox
7. Hagrid
8. *Lassie Come-Home*
9. Charlotte
10. Macavity

Birds

1. White
2. Toco Toucan
3. Emu
4. Oology
5. Ostrich
6. Resplendent Quetzal
7. 'Ode to a Nightingale'
8. Murder
9. Greater Rhea
10. Alfred Hitchcock

Black

1. Black Swan

2. Red
3. Accretion
4. AC/DC
5. Wakanda
6. Ginger
7. Prakash Kapadia
8. Seven
9. Coal
10. Inhospitable sea

Brain

1. Cerebrum
2. Albert Einstein
3. Sperm Whale
4. Common Hawk-Cuckoo
5. Robin Cook
6. Artificial Intelligence
7. Migraine
8. *Limitless*
9. Michelangelo
10. Meningitis

Cartoons and Comics

1. Jasper and Jinx
2. Donald Duck
3. *SpongeBob SquarePants*
4. Bedrock
5. Scooby-Doo
6. Bugs Bunny
7. Popeye
8. Motu Patlu

9. Beagle
10. *Calvin and Hobbes*

Clothes

1. Cardigan
2. Kilt
3. Ecuador
4. Skirts
5. A female ballet dancer
6. Culottes
7. Ties
8. Russia
9. USA
10. George du Maurier

Dance Forms

1. Sattriya
2. Tango
3. Flamenco
4. Manipur
5. Waltz
6. Kathakali
7. Uday Shankar
8. Chhau
9. Bolero
10. Spider

Days of the Week

1. Crash of the US gold market
2. Saturday
3. Friday

4. *Satte Pe Satta*
5. Fat Tuesday
6. Stayin' Alive
7. Monday
8. Solomon Grundy
9. Constantine
10. Wednesday

Diseases and Disorders

1. Chikungunya
2. Aspirin
3. Anorexia
4. Asperger's Syndrome
5. Liver
6. Thalassaemia
7. Small pox
8. Zika
9. Insulin
10. Scurvy

Elections

1. Israel
2. Amitabh Bachchan
3. Ballot
4. Kerala
5. Dropping marbles into bins that have the candidate's picture on them
6. USA
7. President of India
8. Bhutan
9. New Zealand

10. Reese Witherspoon

Environment

1. Ecology
2. Al Gore
3. Chipko Movement
4. Bhopal
5. Chimpanzee
6. *Erin Brockovich*
7. Greenpeace
8. Antarctica
9. *WALL-E*
10. Wangari Maathai

Family Tree

1. R.K. Narayan
2. Shah Jahan
3. Jackson 5
4. Sharmila Tagore
5. Alexander Graham Bell
6. Sister
7. Tipu Sultan
8. Golf
9. William Henry Bragg
10. Dakota Johnson

Famous Addresses

1. White House
2. Amsterdam
3. *A Study in Scarlet*
4. Subhas Chandra Bose

5. Winnie-the-Pooh
6. SpongeBob SquarePants
7. United Nations Headquarters
8. 10, Downing Steet, London
9. Thomas Alva Edison
10. Santa Claus

Famous Detectives

1. Harley Quin
2. Sherlock Holmes
3. Nancy Drew
4. Feluda
5. C. Auguste Dupin
6. Philip Marlowe
7. G.K. Chesterton
8. Hercule Poirot
9. Ellery Queen
10. *The Murder at the Vicarage*

Fashion

1. Coco Chanel
2. Naomi Campbell
3. Hubert de Givenchy
4. *Gandhi*
5. Christian Dior
6. Manish Arora
7. Aiguille stiletto
8. Kanjeevaram
9. Tyra Banks
10. Anna Wintour

Festivals

1. La Tomatina
2. Goa
3. Ahmedabad
4. Songkran
5. Lathmar Holi
6. Rosh Hashanah
7. Deceased ancestors
8. Chhath
9. Wesak
10. Mark Twain

Forts

1. Agra Fort
2. Red Fort
3. Golconda Fort
4. Razia Sultan
5. Humayun
6. Barabati Fort
7. The Gwalior Fort
8. Arunachal Pradesh
9. Shivneri
10. Jhansi Fort

Footwear

1. Raised platform shoes
2. Brogue
3. Mary Jane shoe
4. Mojaris
5. Aglet

6. Mule
7. Brannock Device
8. Wellington
9. Agatha Christie
10. Oxford

Gold

1. Fort Knox
2. Guru Arjan Dev
3. Primate
4. Mohur
5. Sir Francis Drake
6. Pyrite
7. Karnataka
8. Vikram Seth
9. Midas
10. Australia

Harry Potter

1. Ravenclaw House
2. Fluxweed
3. Books
4. Beaters
5. Pensieve
6. Crab
7. Peter Pettigrew
8. Griphook
9. Hungarian Horntail
10. Accio

History

1. World War I
2. Napoleon Bonaparte
3. Rebirth
4. Voltaire
5. Winston Churchill
6. Battle of Plassey
7. John F. Kennedy
8. China
9. Attack on Pearl Harbor
10. Peru

Indian Railways

1. Uttar Pradesh
2. Bangladesh
3. Munshi Premchand
4. Mother Express
5. Mahatma Gandhi
6. West Bengal
7. Palace on Wheels
8. Fairy Queen
9. Udaipur
10. Paul Theroux

Indian Writers in English

1. R.K. Narayan
2. Chetan Bhagat
3. E.M. Forster
4. Arundhati Roy
5. *Flood of Fire*
6. *The White Tiger*

7. *The Golden Gate*
8. Ruskin Bond
9. Dom Moraes
10. Amit Chaudhuri

Indoor Games

1. 22
2. Badminton
3. Queen
4. Turkey
5. China
6. Swimming
7. 50 points
8. Minimumweight
9. Peach
10. Table Tennis

Insects

1. Silverfish
2. Coleoptera
3. Nymph
4. Feet
5. Mosquito
6. Luna moth
7. Luciferin
8. New Zealand
9. Cicada
10. Vladimir Nabokov

Inventions and Discoveries

1. Refrigerator

2. Televisions
3. Alexander Graham Bell
4. Necessity
5. Robert H. Goddard
6. Insulin
7. Laszlo Biro
8. His wife's hand
9. Edwin H. Land
10. Printing press

Islands

1. Greenland
2. Cyprus
3. *Cast Away*
4. Tortoise
5. Sri Lanka
6. Easter Island
7. Gulliver
8. Maldives
9. Borneo
10. Paul Gauguin

Kings and Queens

1. Queen Victoria
2. Thailand
3. Akbar
4. Khalji
5. Tutankhamen
6. Augustus
7. Marie Antoinette
8. Razia Sultan

9. Rani Lakshmibai
10. Alexander the Great

Languages

1. February
2. French
3. Sanskrit
4. *Star Trek*
5. Pali
6. Bhutan
7. S
8. George Orwell
9. Urdu
10. Lingua franca

Last Words

1. Leonardo da Vinci
2. Nostradamus
3. Brute
4. Wife
5. Steve Jobs
6. Light! More light!
7. A.P.J. Abdul Kalam
8. Beethoven
9. 'I'm bored with it all.'
10. Karl Marx

Light

1. Phosphorus
2. 'The Owl and the Pussy-Cat'
3. Aurora Borealis

4. Kohinoor
5. Photons
6. Florence Nightingale
7. Burnt bamboo
8. Cones
9. William Shakespeare
10. Mahatma Gandhi

Magical Numbers

1. Fibonacci numbers
2. Federico Fellini
3. 42
4. Google
5. Seven
6. At sixes and sevens
7. Paper catches fire and burns
8. The Golden Ratio
9. Perfect number
10. Age at the time of the release of the albums

Money

1. China
2. UK
3. Richie Rich
4. Bhutan
5. Jeffrey Archer
6. London
7. Martin Scorsese
8. Shylock
9. Isaac Newton
10. Fool

Music

1. 'I Just Called To Say I Love You'
2. M.S. Subbulakshmi
3. Silver Beatles
4. Led Zeppelin
5. Lady Gaga
6. Kishore Kumar
7. AC/DC
8. Michael Jackson
9. Asha Bhosle
10. John Lennon

National Flags

1. Nepal
2. Brazil
3. Volcanic fires
4. Further Beyond
5. Circle
6. Sun of May
7. France
8. Israel
9. Saffron
10. Egypt

Nobel Prize

1. Literature
2. Boris Pasternak
3. Sweden
4. Youngest Nobel Prize winner
5. Wilhelm Conrad Röntgen

6. Linus Pauling
7. Guglielmo Marconi
8. Literature
9. Aung San Suu Kyi
10. Ronald Ross

Oscars

1. Best Director
2. Reel of film
3. *Mother India*
4. Emil Jannings
5. Cate Blanchett
6. Walt Disney
7. *Patton*
8. Have been given the award posthumously
9. Alfred Hitchcock
10. *Beasts of the Southern Wild*

Painters

1. Pablo Picasso
2. Michelangelo
3. Jamini Roy
4. Satish Gujral
5. Paul Gaugin
6. *The Persistence of Memory*
7. Raja Ravi Verma
8. Leonardo da Vinci
9. M.F. Husain
10. Claude Monet

Precious Stones

1. Pomegranate
2. Opal
3. Ruby
4. Arthur Conan Doyle
5. Africa
6. Sapphire
7. Japan
8. Copper
9. Ireland
10. Seawater

Science Fiction

1. H.G. Wells
2. *2001: A Space Odyssey*
3. *The Martian Chronicles*
4. Isaac Asimov
5. *Frankenstein*
6. *I, Robot*
7. *Dune*
8. Babel
9. Eloi
10. *Nineteen Eighty-Four*

Sequels and Prequels

1. *The Godfather Part II*
2. *Shrek*
3. *Lage Raho Munnabhai*
4. *Mission Impossible*
5. Saul Goodman

6. Mehrangarh Fort
7. *Die Hard*
8. *Star Wars*
9. *The Bourne Legacy*
10. *Bahubali 2: The Conclusion*

Social Media

1. Timeline
2. Snapchat
9. WhatsApp
4. Larry
5. *Gangnam Style*
6. Quora
7. Telegram
8. Myspace
3. LinkedIn
10. Mars Orbiter

Sports in Films

1. The World Cup
2. *Creed*
3. Golf
4. *Bend It Like Beckham*
5. Michael Mann
6. Wrestler
7. *Lagaan: Once Upon a Time in India*
8. *Seabiscuit*
9. Samuel L. Jackson
10. *Titans*

Sweetmeats

1. Trifles
2. Hot Cross Buns
3. Doughnut
4. Pavlova
5. Aabaar Khabo
6. Pick me up
7. Shahi Tukda
8. China
9. Baklava
10. Balushahi

Television

1. *Friends*
2. It is based on a Twitter feed
3. *Desperate Housewives*
4. *Big Brother*
5. *Spelling Bee*
6. Vidya Balan
7. Oprah Winfrey. The name 'Harpo' is 'Oprah' spelled backwards.
8. *CID*
9. *The Big Bang Theory*
10. *Seinfeld*

Tintin

1. *Le Petit Vingtième*
2. Rastapopoulos
3. Professor Calculus
4. President Charles de Gaulle
5. Fox Terrier

6. Sons of the Dragon
7. *Tintin in Tibet*
8. Steven Spielberg
9. Captain Haddock
10. Santu and Bantu

US Presidents

1. Abraham Lincoln
2. Liberia. Its capital is Monrovia.
3. Barack Obama
4. Resigned from office
5. Ronald Reagan
6. John F. Kennedy
7. *The Apprentice*
8. Theodore Roosevelt
9. Jimmy Carter
10. John Adams. His son was John Quincy Adams.

Video Games

1. Brown Box
2. Pac-Man
3. Bowser
4. Tetris
5. Doom
6. The Umbrella Corporation
7. Half-Life
8. Galaga
9. The Legend of Zelda
10. Pong

Wimbledon

1. Martina Hingis
2. Unseeded champion
3. The longest match in the history of the game
4. Mahesh Bhupathi and Leander Paes
5. Women's singles event started
6. Andy Murray
7. Billie Jean King
8. William Renshaw
9. Rudyard Kipling
10. Strawberry

Wonderful Words

1. Spam
2. Dinosaur
3. Robot
4. Boat
5. Singing to pre-recorded music
6. William Shakespeare
7. Paparazzi
8. Malaria
9. White-robed
10. Computer

www.ingramcontent.com/pod-product-compliance
Lightning Source LLC
Chambersburg PA
CBHW020803160426
43192CB00006B/418